The Age of
Diminished Expectations

The Age of Diminished Expectations

U.S. Economic Policy in the 1990s

revised and updated edition

Paul Krugman

The MIT Press
Cambridge, Massachusetts
London, England

The Age of Diminished Expectations was first published in 1990 by the
Washington Post Company as the first book in their series *Briefing Books*.

This book was set in Palatino by The MIT Press and was printed and bound in the
United States of America.

Library of Congress Cataloging-in-Publication Data

Krugman, Paul R.
  The age of diminished expectations: U.S. economic policy in the 1990s /
Paul Krugman.
    p. cm
  Includes index.
  ISBN 0-262-11181-0 (hc). ISBN 0-262-61092-2 (pbk)
  1. United States –Economic policy–1981- 2. Economic forecasting–United States. I.
Title.
HC106.8.K78 1993
338.973'009'049–dc20   93-6411
                                                                          CIP

Contents

Foreword

Today economic writing is better than ever it used to be. But now there is so much of it—often arguing at cross-purposes—that you as an intelligent and motivated reader are more up in the air than ever. What to do?

Needed is a competent guide, prepared by a tested and proved researcher, a briefing book to select the essentials for emphasis and sort them out in a good-sense way that will earn your confidence and understanding. That is a tall order. But Paul Krugman is the economist to try to do the job. And I see that he has succeeded wonderfully well.

I am proud of my generation of policy economists. You know their names: Walter Heller, Milton Friedman, John Kenneth Galbraith, Arthur Okun, Herbert Stein, Peter Drucker, and many more. But, as some sage has said, science progresses funeral by funeral. Paul Krugman is the rising star of this century and the next, and the world beats a path to his door. International finance is his thing, but that is only one of the many strings to his fiddle. The World Bank, the IMF, the Bank of Japan, and the Boston Fed—all seek to tap his fountain of wisdom and new ideas.

The Age of Diminished Expectations is a tour de force. To economists and noneconomists using it as a chart to navigate through the mysteries of inflation and recession, supply-side economics and productivity, floating exchange rates and bouncing stock markets, I say *Bon Voyage!*

Paul A. Samuelson
May 1990

Preface

There are three kinds of writing in economics: Greek-letter, up-and-down, and airport.

Greek-letter writing—formal, theoretical, mathematical—is how professors communicate. Like any academic field, economics has its fair share of hacks and phonies, who use complicated language to hide the banality of their ideas; it also contains profound thinkers, who use the specialized language of the discipline as an efficient way to express deep insights. For anyone without graduate training in economics, however, even the best Greek-letter writing is completely impenetrable. (A reviewer for the *Village Voice* had the misfortune to encounter some of my own Greek-letter work; he found "equations, charts, and graphs of stunning obscurity . . . a language that makes medieval scholasticism seem accessible, even joyous.")

Up-and-down economics is what one encounters on the business pages of newspapers, or for that matter on TV. It is preoccupied with the latest news and the latest numbers, hence its name: "According to the latest statistics, housing starts are up, indicating unexpected strength in the economy. Bond prices fell on the news . . . " This kind of economics has a reputation for being stupefyingly boring, a reputation that is almost entirely justified. There is an art to doing it well—there is a Zen of everything, even short-term economic forecasting. But it is unfortunate that most people think that up-and-down economics is what economists do.

Finally, airport economics is the language of economics bestsellers. These books are most prominently displayed at airport bookstores, where the delayed business traveler is likely to buy them. Most of these books predict disaster: a new great depression, the evisceration of our economy by Japanese multinationals, the collapse of our money. A minority have the opposite view, a boundless optimism: new technology or supply-side economics is about to lead us into an era of unprecedented economic progress. Whether pessimistic or optimistic, airport economics is usually fun, rarely well informed, and never serious.

But what is there for the intelligent reader who wants to be well informed but doesn't want to study for a Ph.D.? The answer, unfortunately, is not much.

In 1989 the *Washington Post* approached me with the idea of writing a short book about the U.S. economy that would be accessible to a nonprofessional public while maintaining intellectual quality. They envisioned this as a pilot for a series of briefing books on a variety of issues, from national defense to the environment, where the specialists and the educated public had ceased to speak a mutually intelligible language. This book is the result.

The title of the book, and its theme, came to me when I tried to put my finger on what airport economics gets wrong. The most important problem with the books at the newsstand, it seemed to me, is that they allow no middle ground between disaster and bliss. Either the economy is about to disintegrate or things will be wonderful—and since the economy rarely disintegrates, those people who are not in a doom-and-gloom mood will usually conclude that we are doing fine. Yet avoiding crisis and doing well are not the same thing.

The simple fact is that the U.S. economy is not doing well, compared with any previous expectation. In the late 1960s, nearly everyone expected the great postwar boom to continue. *Fortune*, for example, predicted in 1967 that real wages would increase by 150 percent by the year 2000. In fact, real wages are no higher now than they were at the time of the article. While a few Americans have prospered to an unprecedented extent, poverty in America has been increasing in both extent and severity. A persistent trade deficit has accelerated America's relative decline in the world economy, to the point where we may well be the third-ranked economic power by the end of this decade.

When will these disappointments come to a head? Quite possibly never—which is why airport economics is so misleading. One can have stability without progress, avoid a depression without achieving sustained economic growth. That has been the basic story of the U.S. economy since the early 1970s, and will probably be its story for the 1990s.

One might have expected that America's economic problems would have come to a head in another way, through the political process. Relative to what almost everyone expected twenty years ago, our economy has done terribly; surely one should have expected a drastic political reaction. I find the lack of protest over our basically dreary economic record the most remarkable fact about America today. Whether it is a sign of our political strength or weakness, it is astonishing how readily Americans have scaled down their expectations in line with their performance, to such an extent that from a political point of view our economic management appears to be a huge success.

This, then, is my theme. We live in an "age of diminished expectations," an era in which our economy has not delivered very much but in which there is little political demand that it do better. In this book I try to document both our economic failures and our successes. More important, I try to explain *why* we are not making more of an effort to do something about our disappointing economy—which comes down in large part to the painfulness of the measures that we would have to take if we were serious about making a difference. And I try to chart the eventual consequences of continuing our present policy.

Along the way this book tries to convey a number of things that professional economists know but that the broader public generally does not. It is important to understand why inflation is less costly to endure and more costly to stop than most people realize; why protectionism, while usually a bad thing, does not cause depressions; how the savings-and-loan debacle was created by misplaced free-market rhetoric. On these and other issues I have found that the simple truth is widely regarded as shocking and heretical.

I hope that America will eventually be roused from its slumber and once again begin to face up to problems instead of letting them slide. The beginning of action must, however, lie in understanding. This book is not a political tract or a call to arms. It is something rarer: an attempt to describe the way things are, and explain why.

Introduction

Bill Clinton's advisers knew what issue could win them the election, and to remind campaign workers they put up a celebrated sign in his Little Rock headquarters: "The economy, stupid." Four years earlier, George Bush was swept into office on a wave of economic contentment; in 1992 he was swept out by a pervasive sense among voters that something was very wrong with the American economy.

But what was bothering voters? The immediate problem was a lack of jobs. In 1990 a seven-year era of declining unemployment rates came to an end, and during the next few years news of major layoffs by once-proud companies became a daily feature of the nation's press. The job drought was particularly shocking because it affected groups and regions that had traditionally been insulated from economic distress. For the first time ever, more white-collar than blue-collar workers were unemployed; the major state most deeply stricken by the new unemployment was California, which once thought itself recession-proof.

Still, unemployment alone could not explain the deeply pessimistic public mood. Even at its peak in August 1992, the unemployment rate was only 7.7 percent, far short of the 10.7 percent peak reached during the previous recession of 1981–82.

By early 1993 the rate had dropped to 7 percent, no higher than in 1984, the year in which Ronald Reagan campaigned on the triumphant slogan "It's morning in America." It's true that any given unemployment rate feels much worse when the economy is on the way down than when it is on the way up, but still dismay over the U.S. economy was out of all proportion to the short-term economic setbacks.

What happened, of course, was that short-term bad news brought to a boil simmering dismay over long-term poor performance. Even during the long economic expansion from 1982 to 1990, the U.S. economy didn't deliver the kind of unambiguous economic progress that previous generations had taken for granted. Although some people became fabulously rich, and a sizable fraction of the population achieved unprecedented affluence, the typical American family and the typical American worker earned little if any more in real terms in 1990 than they did in the late 1970s. Indeed, for the median American worker there has been no increase in real take-home pay since the first inauguration of Richard Nixon. And for Americans in the bottom fifth of the income distribution the years since 1980 have been little short of nightmarish, with real incomes dropping, the fraction of the population in poverty rising, and homelessness soaring.

There are, of course, bright aspects to the picture. During the 1970s and 1980s the American economy was remarkably successful at generating jobs, absorbing the baby boom and the massive movement of women into the paid labor force without a bulge in unemployment. Inflation, which seemed out of control in the 1970s, has subsided to a level that generates little discomfort. An impressive export boom in the late 1980s shrank the massive trade deficits that had created fears of economic crisis in the mid-1980s. The U.S. economy is not without strengths.

Yet overall our economy has done far worse over the past 20 years than anyone would have predicted, and it didn't do much better in the 1980s than in the 1970s. As long as unemployment was falling, many people managed to hold on to a kind of tentative optimism. But as soon as jobs became scarce, a heavy majority of Americans came to agree with what economists had been saying for a long time: we have entered an era in which economic progress has become a doubtful thing. Many Americans feel that they live worse than their parents; even more fear that their children will be worse off than themselves.

In the first edition of this book I coined a name for this new era: the age of diminished expectations. The name has caught on, and is now widely used even by people who didn't read my book.

Although Americans now freely admit that something has gone wrong, there is still great confusion about what the problem is, even among those who try to follow public affairs. Many concerned people are convinced that our difficulties are primarily financial, and could be cured if only the budget deficit could be eliminated. Others are convinced that our problem is essentially one of international competition, from Japan and/or the Third World. There are even a few die-hard supply-siders, who think that if only George Bush had been more like Ronald Reagan the boom years from 1982 to 1989 might have gone on forever.

What even the would-be informed public seems to lack is a sense of how the various policy issues that fill the newspapers and talk shows fit together. During the 1992 campaign Ross Perot promised to fix the economy by "raising the hood and getting to work on it"; but woe to the auto mechanic who starts poking around without a good idea of how a car works! What do the budget deficit and health care costs have to do with the international competitive position of U.S. manufacturing? What does that competitive position have to do with real wages and income distribution? Not many people have a good sense of the

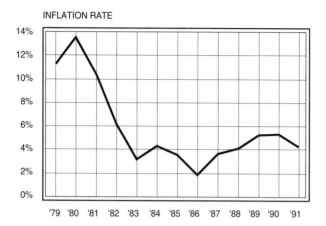

Figure 1
Inflation declined after 1980. . .

Figure 2
. . .and unemployment remained relatively low after its 1982 peak.

MEDIAN FAMILY REAL INCOME

Figure 3
But the real income of typical families stagnated. . .

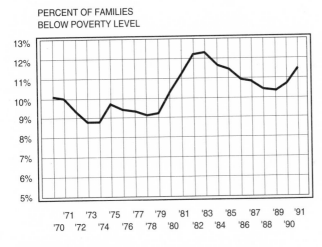

PERCENT OF FAMILIES
BELOW POVERTY LEVEL

Figure 4
. . .and many more people were in poverty in the early 1990s than in the 1970s.

answers to these questions, and many who think they know the answers have them wrong.

Unlike most books written about our economy, then, this book is not a work of advocacy. It is, instead, a guidebook to the economic landscape. Or if you prefer Ross Perot's metaphor, it is an owner's manual for our sputtering economic engine. It attempts, in as plain an English as possible, to explain how things fit together. It will not push for particular answers to our problems, although it will be obvious as we go along that some proposed answers are silly while other have promise (and that some problems have no easy answers).

The book is divided into five parts. The first part addresses the overall economic landscape: the trends that have had the biggest impact on the well-being of large numbers of Americans. A clear view of these trends is important if we want to know how well the economy is doing—but they are not policy issues right now because no seriously debated policy changes would affect them very much.

The second part turns to two aspects of the economy that are widely regarded as problems, and that our government could resolve if it really wanted to: the trade deficit and inflation. As will become clear, however, the government in fact has balked at doing anything significant to reduce either the trade deficit or the rate of inflation—and in this age of diminished expectations, that lack of action has proved acceptable to the public, so long as no crisis results.

The third part of the book discusses a series of narrower policy issues, all interrelated: the budget deficit, health care, monetary policy, the dollar, protectionism and U.S.-Japan relations. All of these issues bear on, and are colored by, concerns about trade and inflation.

No picture of the American economy in the 1990s would be complete without some mention of the extraordinary changes that have taken place in the financial markets. The fourth part of the book describes three "financial follies": the savings and loan crisis, the wild world of corporate finance, and the mysteries of international money.

The book ends with a discussion of America's prospects: What is likely to go wrong (or right) with the U.S. economy? Will the policy sins of the 1980s meet retribution in the 1990s? Will we on the contrary experience a renewed prosperity that makes the doomsayers seem foolish? Or will we simply drift along as we have, neither doing well nor experiencing a crisis?

I   The Roots of Economic Welfare

The well-being of the economy is a lot like the well-being of an individual. My happiness depends almost entirely on a few important things, like work, love, and health, and everything else is not really worth worrying about—except that I usually can't or won't do anything to change the basic structure of my life, and so I worry about small things, like the state of my basement. For the economy, the important things—the things that affect the standard of living of large numbers of people—are productivity, income distribution, and unemployment. If these things are satisfactory, not much else can go wrong, while if they are not, nothing can go right. Yet very little of the business of economic policy is concerned with these big trends.

To many readers this list may seem too short. What about inflation or international competitiveness? What about the state of the financial markets or the budget deficit? The answer is that these problems are in a different class, mainly because they have only an indirect bearing on the nation's well-being. For example, inflation (at least at rates the United States has experienced) does little direct harm. The only reason to be concerned about it is the possibility—which is surprisingly uncertain—that it indirectly compromises productivity growth. Similarly, the budget deficit is not a problem in and of itself; we care about it because we suspect that it leads to low national saving, which ultimately leads to low productivity growth.

So it is important to start our tour of the economy with the right perspective, which is that only the big three issues really matter very much. It is also important to be aware that on two out of the three big issues the American economy has not been performing at all well. Unfortunately, as we review the state of play on these big issues, we will also see that nobody is likely to do much about them.

1   Productivity Growth

Productivity isn't everything, but in the long run it is almost everything. A country's ability to improve its standard of living over time depends almost entirely on its ability to raise its output per worker. World War II veterans came home to an economy that doubled its productivity over the next 25 years; as a result, they found themselves achieving living standards their parents had never imagined. Vietnam veterans came home to an economy that raised its productivity less than 10 percent in 15 years; as a result, they found themselves living no better—and in many cases worse—than their parents.

Although the overwhelming importance of productivity should be obvious, not everyone understands it—or worse, they think that productivity is important for the wrong reasons, such as to help our international competitiveness. So it is worth spending a little while thinking about the issue.

As a starting point, it might be useful to think about how productivity and living standards would be related if the United States did not have any foreign trade. This may seem an outrageous omission, since many people think that productivity is important precisely because we need to be productive to compete on world markets. But this isn't really right—and imagining an economy without trade is a good way to see why.

Suppose, then, that the U.S. economy had no foreign trade so that everything we consume had to be made here. (Incidentally, this isn't such a bad approximation to reality. Even in 1993, with a more integrated world economy than ever before, about 87 percent of the goods and services we consume in the United States will be produced here.) How could we raise our consumption per capita? As a matter of pure arithmetic, there are only three ways:

(i) We could increase our productivity so that each worker produces more.

(ii) We could put a larger portion of the population to work.

(iii) We could put a smaller fraction of our output aside as investment for the future and devote more of our productive capacity to manufacturing goods for current consumption.

Obviously, (iii) is not a long-term way to increase consumption: We can consume more for a while by investing less, but that will surely cut into our ability to consume later. Option (ii) can work for a while if a substantial fraction of the population is unemployed, or if social change brings new groups into the work force; thus rapid growth in the share of the population employed took place as America emerged from the Depression, and again in the 1970s as women entered the work force in large numbers. But over the long term there are evident limits on this: You can increase the share of the population employed from 57 to 62 percent, as we did in the 1970s and 1980s, but you can't increase it to 105 percent.

So the only way in which sustained, long-term growth in living standards can be achieved is by raising productivity. Real consumption per capita in the United States today is about four times what it was at the turn of the century; so is productivity.

Now let's put foreign trade back into the picture. As a trading economy the United States sends part of its output abroad as exports, while importing part of what its people consume. If we can somehow manage to import more without having to export more as well, we can also increase our consumption. This therefore adds two more ways in which per capita consumption can rise:

(iv) We can import more without selling more abroad—which means that we have to borrow or sell assets to pay for the extra imports.

(v) We can get a better price for our exports so that we can afford to import more without borrowing.

Obviously (iv), like (ii), is an option for the short term only, since eventually the borrowing needs to be repaid. As for (v), the problem is how to persuade foreigners to pay more for our goods. The only reliable way to do that is to make our goods better—which is really just a productivity increase under another name.

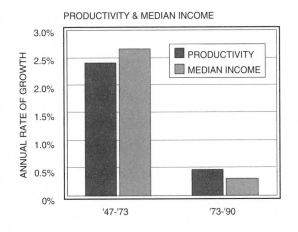

Figure 5
The stagnation of real family incomes during the 1970s and 1980s, like the soaring incomes of the previous generation, was driven by trends in productivity. The doubling of productivity from World War II to 1973 also doubled real incomes; the stagnation of productivity since then has held family incomes down.

Productivity and competitiveness

Many people believe that the most important reason why productivity growth is essential to the U.S. economy is to allow us to compete in the world economy. This is a misconception: productivity growth is no more (and no less) important in an economy open to international trade than in a closed economy.

To see why, it's useful to carry out a thought experiment. First, imagine a world in which productivity in all countries, including the United States, rises at 1 percent per year. What would be the trend in our standard of living? Most people have no difficulty in agreeing that living standards in all countries will rise by 1 percent annually.

Now suppose that productivity growth in the rest of the world rises to 3 percent, while it stays at 1 percent here. Now what is the trend in our living standards? Many people automatically answer that our living standards will stagnate or even decline, because we will have trouble competing. But they're wrong.

The right answer is that our real income will still grow about 1 percent per year. After all, why do we care about productivity growth abroad? It matters only if it affects the quantity of imported goods we receive per unit of goods that we export, that is, the price of our exports relative to the price of our imports (known as our terms of trade). And productivity growth abroad need not hurt our terms of trade—it is equally likely to improve them. There are several ways to see this. One is to note that while growth abroad increases the competition we face, it also expands our overseas markets. Another is to realize that when foreign firms whose products compete with our exports become more productive, those who provide us with imports generally also become more productive. Yet another way to see the point is to realize that faster productivity growth in foreign industries that compete with our exports will generally be reflected in higher wage growth as well, which can more than wipe out any relative cost gain. (These are all different ways of looking at the same story.)

In principle, then, the fact that our productivity growth lags behind growth abroad need not pose a problem. What about in practice? The actual U.S. terms of trade (excluding oil and farm products, which are subject to erratic movements) declined 15 percent from 1970 to 1980, and a further 2 percent from 1980 to 1991. These are very small numbers: since non-oil imports are only 7 percent of GDP, the drag on the U.S. standard of living was less than 1/10 of one percent per year during the 1970s, less than 1/50 of one percent per year after 1980.

In practice, then, the trend in U.S. living standards is determined by our own rate of productivity growth—full stop. International competition has nothing to do with it.

If that's the case, however, what does it mean when people talk about U.S. "competitiveness"?

The answer, sadly, is that it almost always means that they don't know what they are talking about.

So the essential arithmetic says that long-term growth in living standards—like the doubling of our standard of living in the generation following World War II, or the tenfold increase in living standards that Japan has experienced since 1950—depends almost entirely on productivity growth.

Nor are living standards the only thing for which national productivity growth is the decisive factor. Shifts in national power are, in the end, dominated by productivity. Since World War II, productivity growth in Britain has averaged about 1.5 percent a year; in Japan it has averaged 7 percent. Britain won the war, and Japan lost; yet Britain has become a third-rank power, while Japan is on the verge of becoming a first-rank one.

In this light the slowdown of American productivity growth since the early 1970s becomes the most important single fact about our economy. Over the first 70 years of this century, American output per worker rose at an average annual rate of 2.3 percent. During the 1950s and 1960s that rate was 2.8 percent. Since 1970, however, our economy has delivered average

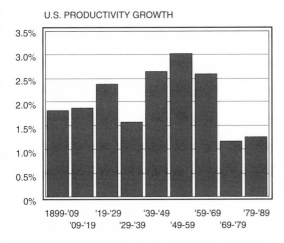

U.S. PRODUCTIVITY GROWTH

Figure 6
The two decades since 1970 have seen the worst U.S. productivity performance of the century.

annual productivity growth of only 1.2 percent. Had productivity over the last 20 years grown as fast as it did for the first 70
years of this century, our living standards would now be at least
25 percent higher than they are.

Compared with the problem of slow productivity growth, all
our other long-term economic concerns—foreign competition,
the industrial base, lagging technology, deteriorating infrastructure, and so on—are minor issues. Or more accurately, they matter only to the extent that they may have an impact on our productivity growth.

Obviously, then, productivity must be a key political issue,
right? Wrong. Economists and business managers occasionally
attempt to make it an issue, but their efforts are largely ignored.
Nor is this simply a matter of public ignorance. Even among the
experts, be they think-tank intellectuals or academic economists,
stagnant American productivity is not a fashionable topic. Of
course it's important, agrees anyone who thinks about it; but
there's nothing much to do about it, so why make a fuss?

This apathy among the experts becomes a little more comprehensible if we ask how economists answer two central questions
about America's productivity slump: Why did it happen? And
what can we do about it? The answer to both is the same: We
don't know.

Start with the first question: Why did productivity growth,
which did so well in the 1950s and 1960s, slow to a crawl thereafter?

A decade ago, when the productivity slowdown was still a
new event, many people thought that it could be attributed to
the energy crisis. The timing was right: The productivity slowdown first became apparent in the five years following the
worldwide oil crisis of 1973. This theory was reinforced by the
fact that productivity slowed everywhere, not just in the United
States. Indeed, the slowdown in West Germany and Japan was

even greater than in America (although growth was faster in both countries both before and after the slowdown).

Many economists were never happy with the energy crisis explanation of the productivity slowdown, for a variety of technical reasons. But that technical debate has now become moot: In the 1980s energy prices fell sharply—in real terms almost back to their 1973 levels. If the energy crisis of the 1970s caused the productivity slump, then the reverse energy crisis of the 1980s should have spurred a corresponding productivity boom. It didn't.

This left economists with a set of explanations for the productivity slump that are little more than sophisticated cocktail party chatter. Conservative economists predictably place the blame on increased government regulation—yet productivity growth has been higher in the highly regulated economies of Western Europe than in the United States, and America's move to deregulation in the 1980s has not borne fruit in any reacceleration of growth.

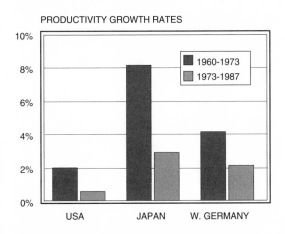

Figure 7
Productivity growth slowed around the world in the early 1970s.

Other economists point to the long-term effects of the social up-heavals of the 1960s on mores, motivation, and the quality of education—what might be called "the *thirtysomething* theory"—though this is not what you call serious economic analysis. As MIT economist Robert Solow has put it, most discussions of poor productivity performance end in "a blaze of amateur sociology."

So we really don't know why productivity growth ground to a near halt. That makes it hard to answer the other question: What can we do to speed it up?

There is a standard economist's answer. Unfortunately, it is fairly depressing. If you want more output, say the economists, provide more inputs. Give your workers more capital to work with, and better education, and they will be more productive. And how are we to do these things? Simple: Suffer. Consume less now, so that more resources are available for investment. Send your children to school for more hours, and pay for the extra teachers and classrooms this requires. Do these things, and though you may be worse off right now, eventually they will pay off and living standards will rise. Ten years from now—or is it 20?—our productivity will be sufficiently higher to make up for present sacrifices.

This is not an answer that inspires fervent political support—especially when one bears in mind that the causes of the productivity slump are not obviously tied to declining investment in plant and equipment or in education. In fact, the American economy placed about as high a share of its resources into investment, and a higher share into education, in the 1970s and 1980s as it did in the 1950s and 1960s. It just didn't work as well. So the orthodox prescription for accelerating productivity growth calls on us to make unprecedented efforts, which will depress our living standards in the short run, to offset an undiagnosed ailment. This is the kind of grim advice that has caused economics to be called "the dismal science."

Can't economists think of anything more cheerful to propose? In the late 1970s, when the productivity slowdown was still news, the question of how to get growth going again called forth enthusiastic advocates of a variety of schemes. The most popular nostrums generally separated along left-right lines. On the left, there were the advocates of "industrial policy": people like Robert Reich and Lester Thurow, who thought that by playing a more active role in the marketplace, the government could accelerate productivity growth. On the right, there were supply-siders: people like Arthur Laffer and Jude Wanniski, who believed that getting the government *out* of the marketplace would unleash a wave of private sector dynamism. Although these groups were at opposite ends of the political spectrum, they had much in common. They were outside the academic mainstream, being either economic heretics like Thurow or Laffer, or noneconomists like Reich (a lawyer) or Wanniski (a journalist). And they offered the political system alternatives to the dreary virtue preached by the economics establishment. They offered free lunches—a chance to invigorate the economy without pain.

When Ronald Reagan was elected, the supply-siders got a chance to try out their ideas. Unfortunately, they failed. It was not an abject failure that left the economy in ruins—the American economy clearly did well enough in the 1980s to satisfy most voters. While there are some economists who think that the policies of the Reagan years stored up disaster for America's future, such predictions of doom carry little political weight. But what supply-side economics in power actually delivered was so far short of what it promised that all the fire went out of the movement. The Republicans won the 1988 election, but the supply-siders were not part of the victory party. Bush's economic team consisted of what the English call "Tory wets": Although they were nominally free-market conservatives, they were unwilling to contemplate further radical surgery on the economy, and they even were tempted to re-regulate in such areas as the environment and financial markets.

The apostles of industrial policy have gotten their own, more limited chance at power under Bill Clinton. Robert Reich is now secretary of labor; the president is known to be an admirer of Lester Thurow's books. But the one-time advocates of a comprehensive industrial policy have toned down their proposals to a far smaller scale. In early 1993 the new administration introduced with some fanfare a set of subsidies and technological .initiatives that might be called an industrial policy, but the sum involved was only $4 billion per year—pocket change in a $6 trillion economy. The political system simply has no appetite for a really major experiment in industrial policy.

So what are we going to do about productivity growth in the United States? Nothing.

Well, not exactly nothing. There are various things the government can do that might accelerate productivity growth without great political risks, from encouraging higher educational standards to supporting a few industry research consortia. These things will be tried, and some of them may even work a little. But the basic political consensus at present is that a low rate of productivity growth is something America can live with. We can hope that something will turn up, and that productivity growth will accelerate of its own accord. As we'll see in chapter 15, there are even signs that our wish may be granted. But we won't do much more than wish.

This, then, is our first big issue. Productivity growth is the single most important factor affecting our economic well-being. But it is not a policy issue, because we are not going to do anything about it.

Income Distribution

Although the typical American family had about the same real income in 1992 as it did in 1980, this was not true of untypical families: the rich and the poor. The best-selling novel of 1988, Tom Wolfe's *Bonfire of the Vanities*, portrayed an America of growing wealth at the top, a struggle to make ends meet in the middle, and growing misery at the bottom. The numbers bear him out. During the 1980s the rich, and for that matter the upper middle class, became a great deal richer, while the poor became significantly poorer.

In making this comparison, it is important to be careful about starting and ending dates. The recovery from 1982 to 1990 raised almost everyone's income, while almost everyone lost during the recession-plagued periods 1979–1982 or 1990–92. As we'll see, however, recessions and recoveries have little to do with either long-term trends or even the policies of the administration in power, so we want where possible to compare years in which the economy as a whole was reasonably prosperous. To get a sense of the trends in inequality, then, it is usual to compare incomes in the late 1970s with those in 1989 or 1990.

The most comprehensive such study of income changes was made by the Congressional Budget Office. (The CBO's numbers have been bitterly attacked by conservative members of

Congress, but they are broadly consistent with other sources of evidence.) Figure 8 shows the CBO's estimates of the percentage changes in the pre-tax income of families in the bottom fifth of the population, the next fifth, and so on up to the top 1 percent.

The growth in inequality is startling. While the incomes of the top 1 percent of families doubled, that of the bottom fifth of families fell by 10 percent. If one bears in mind that tax rates for the well-off generally fell in the Reagan years, while noncash benefits for the poor, like public housing, became increasingly scarce, one sees a picture of simultaneous growth in wealth and poverty unprecedented in the twentieth century.

Even these numbers fail to capture the full extent of what happened, because they miss the real extremes. The real compensation of top executives at major corporations is estimated to have quadrupled from the mid-1970s to 1990; a few thousand investment bankers and real estate developers made astonishing fortunes. At the other end, the amount of sheer misery in America has surely increased much faster than the official poverty rate, as homelessness and drug addiction have spread.

Long-term comparisons of income distribution are fraught with difficulties, but for what it is worth, standard calculations show that the surge in inequality in the United States after 1979 reversed three decades of growing equality, pushing the income shares of the top and bottom categories to their highest and lowest levels, respectively, since 1950. Since measures of inequality in 1950 were magnified by widespread rural poverty, it is probably safe to say that income distribution within our metropolitan areas is more unequal today than at any time since the 1930s.

While some conservatives do not consider income distribution a valid issue for public concern, the changes in that distribution in the 1980s had a far more important effect on people's lives than any deliberate government action. After all, even a disastrous policy blunder is unlikely to lower the real incomes of

50 million Americans by 10 percent; yet that is what happened to the poorest fifth of the population during the 1980s. Not everyone agrees that the soaring inequality of the 1980s was a bad thing, but it is a simple fact that the growth of both affluence and poverty in the 1980s largely reflected changes in the distribution of income, rather than in its overall level.

There are at least two reasons for arguing that the increased inequality of the 1980s changed *overall* welfare for the worse. First, most Americans do care at least a little bit about how well-off others are, and it is hard to argue with the conclusion that an extra thousand dollars of income matters more to a poor family than to someone whose income is already in six digits. Second, the income distribution colors the whole tone of society: A society with few extremes of wealth or poverty is a different, and surely more attractive, place than one with a yawning gulf between rich and poor.

In the long run, income distribution is not as important a determinant of economic well-being as productivity growth, but in the 1980s increasing inequality in income distribution, rather than growth in productivity, was the main source of rising

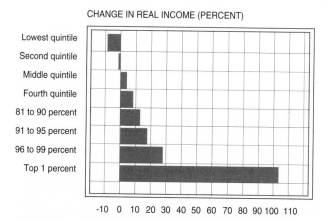

Figure 8
In the 1980s, the poor got poorer while the rich got richer.

living standards for the top 10 percent of Americans. And the 1980s was the first decade since the 1930s in which large numbers of Americans actually suffered a serious decline in living standards.

Yet income distribution, like productivity growth, is not a policy issue that is on the table. This is partly because we don't fully understand why inequality soared, but mostly because any attempt to reverse its trend appears politically out of bounds.

One reason that action to limit growing income inequality in the United States is difficult is that the growth in inequality is not a simple picture. Old-line leftists, if there are any left, would like to make it a single story—the rich becoming richer by exploiting the poor. But that's just not a reasonable picture of America in the 1990s. For one thing, most of our very poor don't work, which makes it hard to exploit them. For another, the poor had so little to start with that the dollar value of the gains of the rich dwarfs that of the losses of the poor. (In constant dollars, the increase in per family income among the top tenth of the population in the 1980s was about a dozen times as large as the decline among the bottom tenth.)

To tell the story of what happened in the 1980s, it is necessary to paint a more complicated picture. At least three separate trends have combined to make our society radically less equal. To begin with, at the very bottom of the scale, the so-called "underclass" grew both more numerous and more miserable. Entirely unrelated, as far as anyone can tell, was a huge increase in the incomes of the very rich. In between, among those who work for a living, the earnings of the relatively unskilled fell while the earnings of the highly skilled rose.

Let's start with the underclass. While there is no generally accepted statistical definition of the underclass, we all know what it means: that largely nonwhite hard core of people caught in a vicious circle of poverty and social collapse. Attempts to measure the size of the underclass, like those of Isabel Sawhill at the Urban Institute, suggest that it began growing during the 1960s, and has continued to grow, perhaps at an accelerating rate, since then. In the 1960s and the 1970s, social programs were expected to cure persistent poverty; in the 1980s, they were widely accused of indirectly perpetuating it. At this point it appears that if you increase spending on the poor, they have more money; if you reduce it, they have less; otherwise, it doesn't make much difference. That is, neither generosity nor niggardliness seems to make much difference to the spread of the underclass. Conservatives argue that the welfare system has reduced incentives and contributed to the growth of the underclass; liberals respond that Reagan's cuts in social spending contributed to the growth of the underclass by making it more difficult for the poor to climb out of poverty. Both could be right. The most important causes of the growth in the underclass, however, like the sources of the productivity slowdown, lie more in the domain of sociology than of economics.

The increased incomes of the rich and very well-off present less of a puzzle than the growth of the underclass. While high incomes have been made in a variety of ways, one source stands out above all: finance. The 1980s were a golden age for financial wheeling and dealing, and the explosion of profits in financial operations has helped swell the ranks of the really rich—those earning hundreds of thousands or even millions a year.

Most Americans live between the stratosphere and the lower depths, and for them the growth in inequality has been yet a different story. First, there was the yuppie phenomenon: The rise of two-income professional couples has increased the number of families with $50,000 or more in annual income. Second, wage differentials among occupations widened: the real wages of blue-collar workers have declined fairly steadily for the past decade, and earnings of highly educated workers have risen rapidly. (The ratio of earnings of college graduates to those of high school graduates declined during the 1970s from 1.5 to 1.3, then rose to 1.8 during the 1980s.)

What we really don't know is why these phenomena have all happened now. The rise of two-income professional couples reflects the lagged effects of the women's movement, plus the aging of the baby boom generation. The surges in pay differentials and in market manipulation are more mysterious. Politics may have had something to do with it. The Reagan years provided a tolerant climate both for tough bargaining with workers and for financial wheeling and dealing. Other forces, like the decline of smokestack America and the consequent restructuring of the U.S. economy, may also have played a role.

Whatever the reasons for soaring inequality in the 1980s, what can policy do about it? In particular, can anything be done about the extremes of wealth and poverty that have emerged in the past decade?

The problem with poverty, as an issue, is that it has basically exhausted the patience of the general public. America launched its War on Poverty in the 1960s—a time of rising incomes and widespread optimism about government activism. This "war" was supposed to be social engineering, not merely charity. It was intended not simply to raise the living standards of the poor, but to help them work their way out of poverty. Yet poverty did not decline. Despite sharp increases in aid to the poor between the late 1960s and the mid-1970s, poverty remained as intractable as ever, and the underclass that is the most visible sign of poverty grew alarmingly. Today, relatively few people believe, as so many did in the 1960s, that government can do much to help the poor become more productive; all that it seems able to do is raise their standard of living by giving them more money (and influential books, like Charles Murray's *Losing Ground*, deny even that).

But if aid to the poor is simply charity, then its political base is nothing more than public generosity. In a time of budget deficits and largely static living standards for the average American, such generosity does not come easily. There are some modest signs of a resurgence of social activism; money may eventually become available to deal with the conspicuous poverty of the homeless; and Congress has made an effort to reform the tax system to help the working poor. But any systematic initiative to raise the incomes of the poor seems unlikely for many years.

As for the rich, a few public policy initiatives might cut down on some of their sources of income. For example, tighter regulation of financial markets might limit the number of people with incomes in the tens of millions, and a cooled-off financial market might indirectly put some limits on executive pay. For the most part, however, the only way to make the rich less so is to tax them. And indeed, in 1993 the new Clinton administration announced plans for tax increases that would fall for the most part on families with incomes over $100,000 per year. These tax increases would roll back part—but only part—of the tax cuts these high incomes received from Ronald Reagan. As we've already seen, however, the bulk of the increase in inequality during the 1980s was a growth in the spread of pre-tax, not post-tax income. So undoing some of Reagan's generosity to the rich would make only a small dent in the trend.

So income distribution, like productivity growth, is a policy issue with little prospect for serious policy action. The growing gap between rich and poor was arguably the central fact about economic life in America in the 1980s. But no policy changes now under discussion seem likely to do much to narrow this gap.

3   Employment and Unemployment

In 1989 only 5.3 percent of the work force was unemployed. This was a slightly lower rate of unemployment than in 1978 (6.0 percent), and somewhat higher than in 1970 (4.8 percent). That may not sound impressive, but in fact it was a remarkable achievement. During the 1970s and 1980s huge numbers of workers entered the U.S. labor force—baby boomers, women, immigrants. The American economy found jobs for almost all of them.

America's success in creating jobs stands out especially well when contrasted with the experience of other countries. In Europe, in particular, virtually no new jobs were created between 1973 and 1985. So even though Europe's labor force grew much more slowly than America's, unemployment increased fivefold.

Why does unemployment matter? Partly because high unemployment means that potentially productive workers are not being used, preventing the economy from producing as much as it might; partly because high unemployment breeds persistent poverty. Beyond this, however, the availability of jobs plays a key role in the way our society hangs together. A society in which young people can routinely expect to get jobs on leaving school, and to remain gainfully employed except for occasional spells for their adult lives, is going to be a very different place from one in which work is a privilege that is unavailable to many people—even if the welfare state is generous to the unemployed, as it is in much of Europe. It is a value judgment to say that a working society, other things equal, is a better society, but it is a value judgment that most Americans would share.

If unemployment is such a bad thing, then, why does the United States content itself with 5 percent or more instead of trying for something lower—say, Sweden's 3 percent, which would add more than two million additional jobs? The answer is not what you might think. It is not that there is insufficient demand for the services of unemployed workers. Creating demand for workers is not usually a problem for the U.S. economy: The Federal Reserve Board can create as much demand as it likes with a phone call. The problem is how to do that without also creating inflation. The principal constraint on reducing unemployment is the fear of the Federal Reserve that too low an unemployment rate will lead to accelerating inflation.

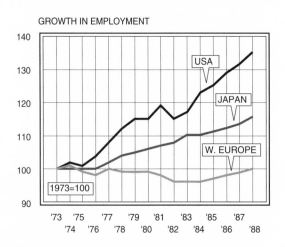

Figure 9
U.S. employment has grown rapidly since the early 1970s; this is in sharp contrast to the experience elsewhere, especially in Europe.

Since the late 1960s, when Milton Friedman and a number of other economists proposed the concept, most economists have agreed that at any given time there is a certain level of unemployment that is consistent with stable inflation. If the government tries to increase demand to drive unemployment below that rate, it will pay the price of accelerating inflation. If the government wants to reduce the inflation rate, it must reduce demand so as to drive unemployment above this rate. The critical rate of unemployment was dubbed by Friedman the "natural rate"; other economists, disliking the suggestion that there was something good about joblessness, have proposed the alternative "nonaccelerating inflation rate of unemployment," or NAIRU.

The logic behind the idea of a NAIRU may be seen by considering the example of an economy where the government is trying to provide very full employment by keeping demand high.

Suppose that when the government starts its program of stimulus, the economy has a history of more or less stable prices. Once demand is increased, however, so that most factories run at capacity and nearly everyone can get a job, there will be a strong tendency for prices to rise. In such an economy firms will feel free to raise prices, and workers will demand wage increases over and above their rate of productivity growth. So in attempting to lower the unemployment rate from, say, 6 to 3 percent, the government might find that its formerly stable prices give way to an inflation rate of, say, 5 percent.

Now maybe the government is willing to make this trade-off. Perhaps it regards 6 percent unemployment as a much more serious problem than 5 percent inflation. Unfortunately, what it will soon find is that the trade-off is not stable. The reason is that persistent inflation gets built into people's expectations. After a few years of 5 percent inflation, workers will come to expect this inflation to continue and will make demands for wage increases over and above it. Firms will set prices higher based on the expectation that their costs and the prices of their competitors will rise at a 5 percent rate until their next price revision. And the government will find that to keep unemployment at 3 percent, it needs to accept not 5 percent inflation, but 10 percent.

If the government still thinks the trade-off is worthwhile, then after a few more years it will find the necessary rate of inflation to be 15 percent—and so on. In the end, the only way to keep unemployment very low will be to accept an ever-accelerating inflation rate. And while 5 percent or even 10 percent inflation may be acceptable, 100 percent or 1,000,000 percent are not.

So to avoid ever-accelerating inflation, the government must accept an unemployment rate that is sufficiently high that workers do not on average demand real wage increases that exceed their productivity growth, and firms do not try to raise their prices faster than their costs. The minimum unemployment rate that will restrain inflation is the NAIRU.

The NAIRU is not an immutable, unchanging feature of the economy. Changes in long-term government policies and in the economy's structure can raise or lower it. For example, restrictive government policies that make it costly for firms to add employees can raise the NAIRU. Many economists blame such policies for "Eurosclerosis"—the persistent rise in European unemployment rates during the period 1970–1985. Demographic changes may also matter: Young workers characteristically have high unemployment rates, so an aging of the work force may lower the NAIRU. The important point, however, is that whatever the NAIRU happens to be at any given time, it places an obstacle to any attempt to expand employment by increasing demand.

Most estimates of the NAIRU for the United States currently place it somewhere between 5 percent and 7 percent. Figure 10 shows an illustration of how these estimates are made. On the vertical axis is the *change* in the rate of increase in consumer prices—for instance, if inflation goes from 3 percent to 5 percent, we indicate this as a value of +2. On the horizontal axis is the rate of unemployment. The scatter of points represents America's experience between 1973 and 1991, with each point representing a particular year. The relationship is not a particularly neat one—this is economics, not physics—but on the whole we see that inflation tended to rise when the unemployment rate was low, to fall when it was high. Notice in particular the points corresponding to the early 1980s, when very high unemployment helped bring a significant reduction in the inflation rate; these points will play a key role in the story when we examine inflation later.

A line plotted through these points crosses zero at about 6.6 percent unemployment; thus, based on the historical record, we would expect that an unemployment rate of less than 6 percent would be associated with accelerating inflation. In fact the

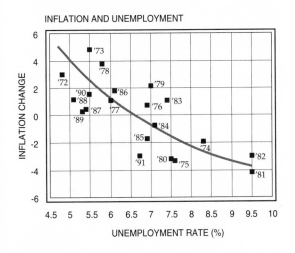

INFLATION AND UNEMPLOYMENT

Figure 10
Inflation tends to rise when the unemployment rate is low, to fall when the unemployment rate is high.

unemployment rate from 1987 to 1990 was closer to 5 percent than to 6 percent, with at best a slight increase in inflation. This is reflected in the fact that the points corresponding to those years lie below the line plotted in figure 10. This may reflect a downward shift in the NAIRU—as baby boomers have become older and women more experienced, the amount of "frictional" unemployment may have declined—or it may just represent luck in what is after all an imprecise relationship.

The important point is that for the United States the NAIRU seems to have been fairly stable, or even falling, during the 1970s and 1980s. This means that there was no long-term tendency for the unemployment rate to increase—and that is quite a tribute to the adaptive ability of the American economy. As we have seen, unemployment rates in Europe rose inexorably for most of the 1970s and 1980s. The U.S. economy might easily have had big problems creating enough jobs for the enormous number of women and baby boomers who entered its labor force over the past decade. With productivity growth so sluggish, and real earnings per worker stagnant or declining, one might have expected worker frustration to lead to large wage demands. As it turned out, America's highly competitive and flexible labor markets made room for all the new entrants and limited wage increases to rates consistent with our slow productivity growth.

After 1990, of course, the story is not quite as happy. The short-term economic management that had kept unemployment gradually falling for the previous few years stumbled, and a recession drove the unemployment rate as high as 7.7 percent before it began declining in the second half of 1992. This rise in unemployment was, however, accompanied by a further decline in inflation—in other words, the unemployment rate in 1991 and 1992 was significantly above the NAIRU. That meant that there was room to increase demand, and no reason not to expect economic recovery to drive unemployment back into the 5-6 percent range once again.

Of course 5-6 percent unemployment is not zero. Shouldn't there be a program to reduce the NAIRU, so that we could have 4 percent or less unemployment? Well, maybe—but there is no widespread agreement among economists about what kinds of policies, if any, would accomplish that goal. Politicians may make a few symbolic efforts, say by offering training to the long-term unemployed, but we can be sure that if the Clinton administration is able to get back to the unemployment rates of the later Reagan years, it will be well satisfied.

II   Chronic Aches and Pains

If you want to ask what really matters for the economic welfare of large numbers of Americans, productivity, income distribution, and employment are probably 90 percent of the story. If you ask what motivates actual legislation and administration initiatives, however, these issues are probably less than 5 percent of the agenda. The reason is not that policymakers don't appreciate the importance of these central issues; it is that they see little within the normal range of policy that they can do about them. Any serious effort to increase productivity growth, or to reverse the sharp increase in income inequality, or to restructure our labor markets to get closer to true full employment, would take a degree of boldness that is rare in economic policy. Attempts to change the economic system in a fundamental way, like Franklin Roosevelt's (or Ronald Reagan's), occur only in the face of economic crisis. And while there are good reasons not to be completely happy about America's economy in the early 1990s, it isn't in crisis—so the big issues don't move actual policy.

But the fact that the most important economic issues are, in effect, out of range does not mean that economic policymaking comes to a halt. It just means that debate focuses on issues that, while less important than, say, productivity growth, are closer to the level that might be a subject of real policy. The issues discussed in the next two chapters, while still not the direct object of legislation, are nevertheless close enough to the ground that current policy discussions are directly affected by the desire to do something about them.

There isn't as much inevitability in the choice of policy problems to discuss as there is in the case of the big issues. Fifteen years ago, energy policy would surely have made the list; today it has faded as a major concern. A decade from now, environmental economics may well be on the list. Right now, however, the two most obvious policy problems to discuss are the trade deficit and inflation.

On these issues, as with the big issues, America's performance has been mixed. We have had persistent trade deficits, but an impressive if not total victory over inflation. If one takes the long view, however, what is most striking about American attitudes toward economic policy is the same thing that is striking about economic performance in general: the willingness to settle for less. If the United States really wanted either balanced trade or stable prices, it could achieve them. But in this era of diminished expectations, nobody expects it even to try.

4   The Trade Deficit

One day recently I had a meeting in New York. Before leaving, I set my Sharp VCR to record a television program I would miss while away. Then I drove my Mazda to the airport, boarded an Airbus A310, and while in transit finished some notes for the meeting on my Toshiba laptop computer. My suit was made in Hong Kong, my coffee cup in Portugal. It is quite possible that my breakfast cereal was the only American-made product I encountered all morning.

This was not a surprising experience in the 1990s, but it would have been very unusual just a dozen years ago. It is sometimes hard to remember that as recently as 1981, the United States exported as large a value of manufactured goods as it imported, and it remained the world's clear leader in high technology. Until the late 1970s, U.S. aircraft and computer manufacturers had no major rivals abroad; imports of foreign automobiles and consumer goods were largely restricted to the low end of the market.

The massive trade deficits that now seem a permanent feature of the U.S. scene emerged quite quickly between 1981 and 1984. In 1981 the U.S. trade picture still looked healthy. Exports of manufactured goods more than paid for manufactured imports, while exports of agricultural goods and earnings from overseas assets more than covered the cost of oil imports. The broadest measure of U.S. trade, the so-called current account of the balance of payments, was in modest surplus, as it had been for most of the century. By mid-1984, however, the current account was in deficit at an annual rate of more than $100 billion, and despite some improvements in the late 1980s, there is little prospect that it will move into balance for years to come. (In fact, it is more likely to increase.)

Many critics of American economic policy in the 1980s point to the trade deficit as evidence that the perceived prosperity of the decade was built on sand. The general public, while sanguine about the economy generally, is worried about the trade deficit; rising public concern led to the passage of the 1988 Trade Act, a law that, while not overtly protectionist, certainly carried a tougher tone than its predecessors. Yet there are also respectable voices claiming that the deficit presents no problem, or even that it is a sign of American strength. Before we even ask why the United States has begun to run a trade deficit, we need to ask why the trade deficit matters.

Why worry about the trade deficit?

Ask the man in the street why a trade deficit is a bad thing, and he will probably answer that it costs America jobs. The point seems obvious enough: If we spend more on imports than foreigners spend on our exports, the result is reduced demand for American labor. The immediate job costs of international competition are easy to understand: plants closed because of competition from imports, workers laid off because of the drying up of export markets. At first glance the numbers can seem very impressive. Consider, for example, the situation in 1990. In that year the United States ran a current account deficit of $98 billion, about 1.8 percent of national income. If we could somehow have kept those dollars at home, the extra demand would have been enough to employ about two million more workers. It is natural to imagine that those two million "lost jobs" are the crux of the problem.

Yet focusing on the employment effects of the trade deficit is not only misleading—it is slightly more than 100 percent wrong. America's trade deficit problem has nothing to do with jobs. As we have seen, the 1980s were actually a time of quite satisfactory job creation. New jobs created in sectors that are insulated from international competition, such as services, far outpaced any job losses in export or import-competing sectors. Not only did the United States do very well at creating jobs in the 1980s despite the ballooning trade deficit, it would have done little if any better—indeed, probably a bit worse—had the trade deficit somehow been prevented.

The reason is that the amount of employment offered in the U.S. economy is normally limited by supply, not demand. It's

Figure 11
The U.S. economy generally ran small surpluses on its current account, the broadest measure of its international trade, until 1981. In the 1980s, however, the nation plunged into a deep trade deficit. This deficit peaked in 1987 and has declined since then, especially when measured as a share of national income.

not very hard to increase demand: The problem is that increasing demand too much leads to inflationary pressures. Driving the unemployment rate below 5 to 6 percent will lead to accelerating inflation. In 1990, U.S. unemployment was, if anything, at the low end of the safe range, so we could not have had fuller employment without higher inflation.

Imagine that in 1990 America could somehow have eliminated its trade deficit at a single stroke—say, by imposing quotas on imports. This would have added to the current demand for labor the demand for another two million workers to fill the jobs currently "lost" because of the deficit. But would employment really have risen by two million? Of course not. First of all, the United States does not have two million suitable workers available (or the plant capacity to employ them). America in 1990 was not like America in 1938, with a huge reserve army of easily employable workers ready to go to work given sufficient demand. Most of the five million or so unemployed were either unskilled or part of the inevitable "frictional" unemployment that occurs as workers change jobs or outmoded plants close. The main effect of an increase in demand would have been not to increase employment but to bid up wages. To put it another way, adding two million jobs, if we could have done it, would have driven the U.S. unemployment rate down to around 3 percent. But that isn't possible, or at any rate not for very long: At that low an unemployment rate, inflation would begin to accelerate rapidly.

In reality, of course, that wouldn't happen. The Federal Reserve Board would raise interest rates to choke off demand and cool down the economy. Since the economy already had more or less as many workers employed as it could manage without inflationary pressure, this offset would destroy roughly as many jobs as eliminating the trade deficit would create. They wouldn't be the same jobs: Construction and service workers would be laid off while manufacturing workers were called back. But overall employment would not rise.

Attempts to reduce the trade deficit might even have led indirectly to a *fall* in employment, at least for a while, as the government either drove down the exchange value of the dollar or restricted imports, both of which are inflationary in their own right. To keep inflation under control would therefore have taken a little extra tightening on the domestic side. So we would probably have had slightly fewer jobs without the trade deficit than we do with it.

Alert readers will have noticed that this argument was carefully applied to 1990—a year in which the U.S. economy was at or below the NAIRU. But what about when the economy is in a recession, as it was in 1992? Didn't the trade deficit cost jobs then?

The answer here is a little more complicated. Other things equal, the United States would have had lower unemployment in 1992 if it had had a smaller trade deficit. This was because the U.S. economy as a whole was suffering a shortfall in demand,

U.S. NET INTERNATIONAL INVESTMENT POSITION

Figure 12
The trade deficits of the 1980s changed the United States from the world's largest creditor to its largest debtor, reversing the results of 60 years of investment abroad in only four years.

and reducing the trade deficit is one way to increase demand. But there are lots of other ways to increase demand, such as cutting interest rates, reducing taxes, or increasing public spending; all of these are pleasant things to do in their own right. The constraint on doing enjoyable things to increase demand is the risk that we will overdo it and create inflation problems—and a smaller trade deficit would increase that risk.

The point is that although the U.S. economy does sometimes stumble into recessions, our ability to keep unemployment down is ultimately limited by supply, not demand. A lower trade deficit might seem to mean more jobs in a particular year, but over the long run the trade deficit and the average rate of unemployment are pretty much unrelated.

If the trade deficit doesn't cost jobs, why worry about it? One answer is that we shouldn't. Herbert Stein, Chairman of the President's Council of Economic Advisers under Richard Nixon, has flatly declared the trade deficit to be a "nonproblem." A significant minority of economists agrees with him. Some even believe that it represents a sign of America's strength. But even these optimists would concede that the trade deficit does have a cost: a gradual mortgaging of future U.S. income to foreigners.

After all, the United States does not get its imports for free. When we buy more goods and services from foreigners than we sell to them, we must give the foreigners something else to cover the difference. What we give them is assets: The U.S. trade deficit in the 1980s was financed by a steady sale of American assets—stocks, bonds, real estate, and, increasingly, whole corporations to foreigners.

The U.S. Department of Commerce regularly reports an estimate of what it calls the U.S. net international investment position: the difference between the value of American assets abroad and foreign assets in the United States. That position has been in the black since World War I, when Britain liquidated many of its holdings here and borrowed heavily from U.S. banks to finance its war effort. The U.S. net investment position grew substantially in the 1950s and 1960s as U.S. corporations went multinational. Even during the 1970s the United States continued to invest more abroad than foreigners did here.

But that investment position quickly evaporated. At the end of 1983 our claims on foreigners were still worth $268 billion more than foreign claims on the United States by the end of 1991 the situation was more than reversed, with foreign assets here exceeding our assets abroad by $382 billion.

What's wrong with being a net debtor? There is one definite cost. There are also some vaguer risks.

The definite cost is, by definition, that you owe people money. From now on, the United States will be obliged to deliver a stream of interest payments to foreign bondholders, rents to foreign landowners, and dividends to foreign stockholders. The numbers are fairly staggering. In 1981 U.S. net investment income from abroad was $34 billion; in 1989 it was negative; and the number will continue to worsen as foreigners expand their U.S. holdings. Our payments to foreigners are a direct drain on our resources, and the longer the trade deficits continue, the larger this drain will become.

But America is a huge country; it can shrug off burdens that would crush smaller nations. The spectacular decline in our net investment income since 1981, measured as a share of GNP, amounts to about a 1.5 percent drain on our economy—not a trivial number, but hardly ruinous. If the United States were to continue to sell assets at current rates, the burden of paying foreign investors could rise by an additional 2 to 3 percent of GNP by the end of the century. Again, this is serious, but no cause for panic. The United States could continue to run trade deficits as big as that of 1989 for a long time before the payment burden becomes unsupportable.

But what about the risks? The big economic risk is that as the United States becomes a massive net debtor it will be exposed to financial crises whenever the confidence of foreign investors is shaken. This is what happened to most of Latin America at the beginning of the 1980s. Banks lent the Latin nations large sums for a decade, then abruptly cut off the flow when their confidence began to waver, precipitating an economic crisis. The vision of the United States as a giant Argentina may be unlikely, but no one should dismiss it out of hand.

The other risks are political. First, there is at least some case to be made that growing foreign ownership of U.S. assets compromises our national sovereignty. We tended to dismiss this argument as patently silly when we were the foreign investors who wanted to invest in other countries. Now that the shoe is on the other foot, it seems more compelling. Second, both the trade deficit and the growing foreign stake here tend to feed crude forms of economic nationalism at home, increasing the risks of a trade war. In fact, it was primarily concern over growing protectionist pressure that led the Reagan administration to start talking down the dollar in 1985.

The measurable costs of the trade deficit, then, are serious but not devastating. The risks are uncertain but worrisome. There isn't any reason to panic about the trade deficit, but getting it down would make everyone breathe a little easier.

But before we start talking about bringing the trade deficit down, we need to ask why we have a deficit in the first place.

Why the trade deficit?

In 1982 Martin Feldstein, the Harvard professor newly appointed Chairman of the President's Council of Economic Advisers, found a new reason to condemn the emerging budget deficit. At a time when most critics of that deficit worried that it would lead to inflation, or perhaps to high interest rates, Feldstein argued that it would lead to something quite different: unprecedented *trade* deficits. Initially his audiences were bemused. Over time, however, as the budget and trade deficits mounted together, the idea of "twin deficits" became a cliché—as well as a target for bitter attack.

Feldstein was, of course, deliberately oversimplifying. His emphasis on the linkage between the two deficits had two purposes: first, to persuade his "what-me-worry" political masters that they should do something about the budget deficit; and second, to answer protectionists who blamed the U.S. trade deficit on unfair foreign trade practices. Today, few economists believe in a simple one-to-one linkage between the budget and trade deficits. Yet a revised version of the "twin deficit" story is still the best explanation for the emergence of unprecedented trade deficits in the 1980s.

The basic story runs as follows: Beginning in 1981, U.S. national saving began to fall sharply. Only part of that fall was a result of the budget deficit—hence the need to qualify the "twin deficit" view a bit—while part of it represented a change in the behavior of households. In any case, what happened was that U.S. national saving began falling well short of U.S. investment demand, which remained strong. If the U.S. economy had not had access to world capital markets, this saving shortfall would have produced a crunch that pushed interest rates sky-high. Instead, the United States was able to turn to foreigners to fill the gap. Much of U.S. investment was financed, not out of our own savings, but through the sale of assets to foreigners.

As a matter of straightforward accounting, the United States always buys exactly as much as it sells from the rest of the world. If it sells foreigners more assets than it buys, it must correspondingly buy more goods than it sells. So the emergent U.S. dependence on foreign capital to finance its investment had as an inevitable counterpart the emergence of a trade deficit. The ultimate cause of the trade deficit therefore lies in a decline in U.S. saving—partly, but not entirely, due to the budget deficit.

Although this mainstream story is now widely accepted, many readers may feel that it is missing something. Where are all the real things that affect international trade? What happened to the dollar? What happened to U.S. competitiveness? Don't these have something to do with the trade deficit, too?

The answer is that they do, and then again at a deeper level they don't. That is, at any point in time, when we discuss the U.S. trade deficit, the level of the dollar and the international competitiveness of U.S. industry clearly matter. The ups and downs of the dollar, in particular, have been spectacular since 1980. When the dollar rose against the currencies of our major competitors in the first half of this decade, it sharply raised the prices of U.S. goods relative to foreign, playing a key role in encouraging imports and discouraging exports. Some of this effect was reversed when the dollar fell again after 1985. Yet even though exchange rates play a crucial role in international trade, at a deeper level capital flows are the real story.

The relationships among capital flows, exchange rates, and the U.S. trade balance have become the subject of a peculiarly nasty debate in recent years—peculiar, because the subject is relatively technical and straightforward. Yet hardly a week goes by without an angry debate between mainstream economists, who assign great importance to the exchange rate, and their critics.

One line of criticism comes from the right. Many conservatives believe that the world should return to a gold standard—that the value of each currency should be fixed in terms of gold. Since this would also fix the values of currencies in terms of each other, these conservatives are uncomfortable with the idea that changes in exchange rates may sometimes play a useful role. So they welcome the arguments of academics like Stanford's

Why devaluation is sometimes a good idea

At a basic level, the United States has a trade deficit because it spends more than it earns, and Germany and Japan have trade surpluses because they earn more than they spend. That's why any attempt to solve trade imbalances simply by shifting demand from foreign to U.S. goods will fail. but if this is the case, why bother with expenditure-switching policies at all? Why is devaluing the dollar sometimes a good idea?

The reason is that trying to solve the U.S. trade deficit just by cutting U.S. spending and raising demand abroad will not lead to the right *kind* of demand. Despite the rapid increase in international trade over the past 40 years, the world economy is still far form being perfectly integrated. Most of the income of U.S. residents is spent on goods and services produced here; the same is true of Europe and Japan. As a result, most of a reduction in U.S. expenditure will be reflected, other things equal, in a fall in demand for U.S. goods and services; only a small fraction of an increase in expenditure in Europe or Japan will be spent on U.S. products.

To see the problem this causes, consider the example illustrated in the accompanying table. Imagine that the United States reduces its spending by $100 billion, while the rest of the world (ROW) simultaneously increases its demand by the same amount. Does this translate smoothly into a $100 billion reduction in the trade deficit? Unfortunately, it does not. At least $80 billion of the reduction in U.S. spending is likely to represent a fall in demand for goods and services produced here, with only $20 billion representing a fall in demand for imports. Meanwhile, no more than $10 billion of the rise in spending of the rest of the world is likely to be spent on U.S. goods, with $90 billion spent on ROW products. The result is therefore a net reduction in demand for U.S. products of $70 billion, and an equal increase in demand for ROW products. Instead of a smooth reduction in the U.S. trade deficit, we would get a combination of recession in the United States and inflation abroad. To make the adjustment work, some way has to be found to *switch* $70 billion in spending from ROW to U.S. products. The easiest way to do this is to lower the foreign exchange value of the dollar, which makes U.S. goods cheaper to ROW residents and ROW goods more expensive to U.S. residents.

The lesson of this example is that while devaluing the dollar cannot by itself solve a trade deficit, it can be crucial as part of a deficit-reduction strategy.

	Total demand	Demand for U.S. products	Demand for ROW products
United States	−100	−80	−20
ROW	+100	+10	+90

Ronald McKinnon, who declares that exchange rates are irrelevant to trade.

Other critics come from the left—people who want an active government role in promoting exports and limiting imports, and who dislike the idea that a market mechanism like the exchange rate can do the job. They therefore like the arguments of pundits such as the *New Republic*'s Robert Kuttner, who wants us to use a tough trade policy to bring our trade deficit down, and who accuses the advocates of a low dollar of wanting to balance trade by cutting American wages.

As usual, the intellectual debate has been warped by the political imperatives of the moment—a distortion that takes place all the more readily because it takes a little sophistication to understand what the exchange rate does and does not do.

The important thing to grasp is that the exchange rate is a crucial part of the *mechanism* that determines the trade balance, without being an independent *cause* of the trade balance. If this sounds unduly metaphysical, consider the following analogy. Think of the U.S. trade balance as an automobile. The exchange rate is not that car's engine—it is more like the drive shaft, with desired capital flows providing the motive power. In other words, changes in the exchange rate play a crucial role in translating changes in desired capital flows into changes in the trade balance, but the root cause of the trade imbalance lies elsewhere.

America's experience in the first half of the 1980s provides a good example. National saving fell—that is, consumption spending increased as a share of national income. But investment spending remained high, because an inflow of foreign capital took the place of the reduced flow of domestic saving. So overall spending in the U.S. economy rose faster than national income. The only way for an economy to spend more than it earns, however, is to import more than it exports—to run a trade deficit. So it was inevitable that the United States would develop a large trade deficit.

It was not inevitable that this trade deficit would emerge via a strong dollar. The Federal Reserve could have expanded the supply of dollars to keep the exchange rate low. But this would have led to an inflationary boom that sucked in imports (an experience that Britain has just had). As it turned out, however, the Federal Reserve kept inflation down by raising interest rates, which made dollar-denominated assets attractive to foreigners and so led to a rise of the dollar against other currencies. This rise in the dollar, by making U.S. goods expensive compared with foreign, then led to the emergence of the unprecedented trade deficits that were the counterpart of the capital inflows. The point is that while the rise of the dollar was a central part of the story as it actually played out, it is still correct to say that the U.S. trade deficit was essentially caused by the fall of national saving, which led to massive imports of capital.

What about competitiveness? It is obvious to everyone that the once-vaunted U.S. superiority over other nations in technology and quality has eroded and perhaps vanished over the past decade. Doesn't this loss of superiority help explain the rise in our trade deficit? The answer is no. If U.S. national saving had remained high, the loss of competitive advantage would not have led to a trade deficit. It would instead have led to a fall in the dollar, which would have compensated for the loss of technology and quality by making U.S. goods relatively cheaper. This is what happened in the 1970s. The United States had about the same trade balance at the end of the 1970s as it did at the beginning, but with a much lower dollar. This isn't to say that a dollar that declines every year is without costs. Competitiveness does matter—but not for the trade deficit.

We'll come back to exchange rates and competitiveness when we look at dollar policy in chapter 9. For now, the important thing to recognize is that the root cause of the trade deficits of the 1980s was America's low national saving rate, which led it to

import large quantities of capital. The next question is: What can
be done about it?

Can the trade deficit be eliminated?

Can the United States eliminate its trade deficit? Of course it can.
When it really wants to (or really has to), virtually any country
can run a trade surplus. Most Latin American countries quickly
shifted from large trade deficits to large trade surpluses when
the debt crisis struck in the early 1980s. The United States may
not want to emulate that experience, but it shows that trade
deficits are not immutable facts. If America continues to run a
trade deficit, it is because it chooses not to take the steps that
would eliminate it.

The solution to a trade deficit has two parts. Expenditure
must be both *switched* and *reduced.* Somehow people must be
persuaded to switch their demand from foreign to U.S. goods—
either by reducing the value of the dollar or by imposing tariffs
and import quotas. But this isn't enough. There must also be a
policy to reduce the level of domestic demand, so that the
expenditure-switching policies don't just feed inflation.

That, of course, is the problem. We can all agree that it would
be nice if Americans could sell more to foreigners and buy less,
although we may argue about how best to arrange that happy
event. Reducing domestic demand is another matter.
Expenditure reduction hurts, and there is only one reliable way
to do it: balance the federal budget. Since the political system
has no intention of doing that, there is nothing much the United
States can do to eliminate its trade deficit.

It's important to understand why both switching and reducing are needed to eliminate the trade deficit. Let's therefore
imagine the consequences of two alternative strategies for reducing the trade deficit *without* a cut in domestic demand: an

aggressive effort to drive the dollar down, making U.S. goods cheaper on world markets; and a protectionist policy that imposes new restrictions on U.S. imports.

There is no question that the government—or more accurately the Federal Reserve—could drive the dollar down if it wanted to. All it has to do is increase the supply of dollars. The resulting fall in the foreign exchange value of the dollar would certainly help U.S. exporters and make it easier for American firms to compete with imports at home.

Unfortunately, there is a side consequence of printing dollars: inflation. Any policy that tries to drive the dollar down other than by reducing our need for foreign capital will necessarily feed inflation. This is an unwanted consequence in and of itself, and it also undermines the initial objective of the policy, because inflation reduces the competitiveness of U.S. producers at any given exchange rate. The eventual result of an effort to drive the dollar down will be to raise U.S. prices by roughly the same proportion as the dollar falls, so that U.S. competitiveness is unaffected. The result, then, would be inflation with no gain on the trade front.

A protectionist policy could certainly reduce U.S. imports. But if U.S. savings have not been increased, lower imports will mean a lower supply of dollars to the foreign exchange market and thus a stronger dollar; the rise in the dollar will cut into exports and encourage increases in whichever imports are not restricted. The dollar will probably rise enough to just about eliminate the favorable impact of the import restrictions on the trade balance. The Federal Reserve could, of course, prevent the dollar from rising by printing more dollars—but this merely brings back the inflation problem.

The moral of both of these scenarios is fairly simple. There isn't much that the United States can do about its trade deficit simply by trying to encourage exports or discourage imports.

The only way to cut the trade deficit successfully is to accompany export-promoting and import-cutting measures with domestic policies that reduce domestic demand—in effect making room for a trade improvement.

But how can we reduce domestic demand? For practical purposes, only one course of action is open: cutting the budget deficit. Even if you don't believe the simple "budget deficit equals trade deficit" formula that Feldstein made so popular, there are no plausible ways for the federal government to make room for balanced trade except by balancing its budget. This might not work: Even balancing the budget might fail to eliminate the trade deficit (we'll spend more time on this in chapter 7). But it is the only plausible policy. It is also not going to happen.

So the solution to the trade deficit is both clear and unacceptable. Eliminate the budget deficit and drive the dollar down (or impose new restrictions on imports), and probably (though not certainly) the trade deficit will shrink rapidly. But since we have no intention of eliminating the budget deficit, the solution isn't available. Implicitly, the United States has decided to live with its trade deficit.

5   Inflation

The dramatic reduction in inflation in the first half of the 1980s was the great triumph of U.S. economic policy in the decade. At the end of the 1970s the U.S. inflation rate seemed out of control. In 1979, for the first time ever in peacetime, consumer prices rose at a double-digit rate (12 percent); in 1980 the inflation rate rose to 13 percent. Few would have predicted that by 1986 the inflation rate would have been just 4 percent—a rate that persisted until the decade's end.

Yet the victory was far from total. Inflation was stabilized, not eliminated, at rates that would have been regarded as unacceptable a generation ago. Public officials insist that inflation can and will be gradually eliminated. But in fact the inflation rate has changed little for the past eight years. Even though inflation eased in the 1980s while the trade deficit went up, current U.S. policy toward both is much the same: to live with what we have.

Why isn't eliminating inflation a priority? For the same reasons that reducing the trade deficit isn't a priority: because the costs of living with inflation are not too high, and the costs of bringing it down look unacceptable. Given the diminished expectations of the American people, getting inflation down to the point where prices only double every 20 years is good enough.

The costs of inflation

Why is inflation a bad thing? That's a surprisingly hard question to answer. In fact, it is one of the dirty little secrets of economic analysis that even though inflation is universally regarded as a terrible scourge, most efforts to measure its costs come up with embarrassingly small numbers.

To see why, it may be useful to ask a superficially silly question: Are the British better off because they have such a valuable currency? The pound sterling is worth about $1.50 on foreign exchange markets. This means that, on average, the price rung up for any given item on an American cash register is about 1.5 times as high as the price rung up for the same item on a British cash register. Would we be better off if we made a dollar equal in value to a pound? Of course not. If the dollar were worth more, everybody's income in dollar terms would be that much less.

Now suppose that over the next ten years the overall level of U.S. prices were to rise by 50 percent (not a bad guess). Will this hurt us? Arguably it will do no more harm than deciding to use dollars instead of pounds to calculate prices. What harm does it do if all prices rise by 50 percent, if all income rises by the same amount? In real terms everyone will be in the same position, so nobody has actually lost.

That isn't the whole story, of course. But it is important to realize that to an important extent inflation is, as economists like to say, "neutral"—a general rise in prices need not affect anything real.

Where does the harm from inflation come from, then? The answer is that what really hurts the economy is not higher prices as such but the fact that prices are constantly changing, which can distort decisions and reduce the economy's efficiency.

The most concrete cost of inflation is that it discourages the use of money. In economies experiencing "hyperinflation" (that is, inflation at an annual rate in the thousands of percent), people may stop using money altogether, resorting to barter or to the use of black market foreign currency to avoid holding cash that loses value by the hour. This obviously cripples a modern economy. For an economy with inflation of 10 percent or less a year, however, the demonetizing effect of inflation is trivial.

More significant for the United States is the fact that inflation causes problems for the tax system. Inflation creates paper gains for the owners of assets that do not represent gains in real value—yet these paper gains are taxable, and so inflation may discourage saving and capital formation. On the other hand, inflation also creates paper losses for firms that have a lot of debt, which helps reduce their taxes—and it therefore encourages increased corporate debt, a phenomenon that worries many people.

Inflation may harm investment in other ways. In an inflationary world, accounting measures of corporate performance become confusing: some reported profits and losses are really just inflation illusion. Investors may therefore have difficulty evaluating firms in an inflationary world, and firms may have difficulty evaluating their own investment plans; so inflation may degrade the quality of business decisions.[1]

Lastly, unexpected inflation can produce windfall losses to individuals and institutions; even if losses are matched by gains elsewhere, they can be disruptive. The most dramatic example is that of the savings and loan industry, where fluctuations in the

---

1. It is sometimes argued that fear of inflation discourages investment by keeping long-term interest rates high. This is half right. Expectations of inflation do keep interest rates high; but they do so precisely because borrowers are willing to pay higher rates when they expect to repay in dollars of reduced purchasing power. In fact, if we were to eliminate inflation—which would be a surprising development—the result would be catastrophic to all those firms and individuals who have borrowed long-term money at interest rates based on the assumption that inflation will reduce the real burden of repayment. So the direct effect of inflation on nominal interest rates does not systematically increase the real cost of borrowing.

inflation rate conspired with regulatory blunders to produce a public policy disaster.

All of these costs of inflation are, however, either small or avoidable. The United States does not, at its current inflation rate, run any risk of becoming a barter economy. The tax problems caused by inflation could be met with tax reform instead of lower inflation. Accounting standards could be revised to take account of inflation. And the costs of past surprises in inflation are mostly behind us. Any future surprises will come if inflation is eliminated, not if it continues at present rates.

As far as economic analysis can tell us, a steady inflation rate of 3 or 4 percent does very little harm—and even a rate of 10 percent has only small costs.

Why, then, was a victory over inflation so important? Partly because many people *think* that inflation hurts them. The costs of higher prices on the checkout line are obvious, while the role of inflation in allowing everyone to get bigger wage increases is less so. So there may be a public perception that inflation reduces living standards even when it really doesn't.

More important, though, is the difference between a steady inflation rate and one that is accelerating. In the days of Jimmy Carter, when inflation seemed to set a new record each year, there was a widespread sense that things were out of control— this year 13 percent, next year 20 percent, maybe the year after that hyperinflation. It was crucial to the credibility of economic policy that some kind of victory over inflation be won.

It turned out, however, that reducing inflation was not cheap. Indeed, it was almost inconceivably expensive.

The costs of disinflation

In 1980 there were many economists and politicians who thought that double-digit inflation was incurable. They were wrong. On the other hand, there were some economists, including the first Reagan administration's advisers, who thought that victory over inflation would be cheap. They were also wrong. What happened was that the conventional *economic* wisdom, which said that reducing inflation would be very costly, proved right; but the conventional *political* wisdom, which said that these costs would never be paid, proved wrong.

How was limited victory over inflation won? Part of the answer is pure luck. In the late 1970s the inflation rate was swollen by a series of events that had little to do with economic policy. Most important, the fall of the Shah of Iran set in motion a temporary quadrupling of oil prices. Additional damage was done by soaring world food prices, driven by such disparate events as harvest failures in the Soviet Union and the disappearance of the Peruvian anchovies. In the mid-1980s, by contrast, the price of oil collapsed, and world prices of most other raw materials declined. To distinguish between these kinds of transitory events and more fundamental trends in inflation, many economists like to measure inflation not by the change in the consumer price index per se, but by looking at an "underlying" rate that leaves out changes in food and energy prices. When we look at this underlying rate, the late 1970s don't look quite as bad and the mid-1980s don't look quite as good. Still, the progress is impressive: Underlying inflation was brought down from about 10 percent in 1980 to about 4 percent in 1988.

There is no economic mystery about how this was achieved. America brought down its inflation the time-honored way: by engineering a sustained period of low output and high unemployment as a way of inducing workers to reduce their wage demands and firms to moderate their price increases. During the 1980s the United States, as a deliberate policy, put its economy through the deepest recession since the 1930s. If there is a puzzle, it is political: Why was the system willing to pay the enormous cost of this policy?

Recall the NAIRU. Any attempt to keep the unemployment rate below the NAIRU for a sustained period will lead to accelerating inflation. The converse is also true: To reduce the inflation rate, it is necessary for the economy to experience sustained unemployment rates above the NAIRU. Since a high unemployment rate corresponds to an economy running below its capacity, this means that to reduce inflation, the economy must sacrifice output.

Most estimates suggest that reducing inflation is very expensive indeed. To reduce the inflation rate by one percentage point a year, say the standard estimates, the economy has to run something like four percentage points below capacity. In another piece of ugly but useful economics jargon, this is known as the "sacrifice ratio": You have to sacrifice four points of output to reduce inflation by one point. That's a high price, even though the loss of output is only temporary while the reduction in inflation is permanent (unless you throw the gains away with irresponsible policies at a later date). It's hard to believe that anyone would be willing to pay the price of bringing the inflation rate down from 10 percent to 4 percent.

Yet that's what the United States did. Figure 13 shows the picture, which is about as clear as anything in economics. It shows two lines. One line represents "trend" output: a projection of what the U.S. economy would have produced during the 1980s if it had continued to grow steadily at the same 2.4 percent rate at which it grew from 1973 to 1979. This trend line represents a rough estimate of what the U.S. economy could have produced if it had been running at more or less full capacity. The other line shows the actual gross national product, which fell sharply below the trend line from 1979 to 1982, and did not get back close to the trend line until 1987. The gap between these two lines—the difference between what the economy could have produced and what it actually produced—represents a rough estimate of the cost of America's war on inflation. This gap peaked at 10 percent of GNP in 1982 and averaged 3 percent over the seven years from 1980 to 1986. That is, the U.S. economy sacrificed more than 20 percent of a year's GNP to bring inflation down. This is a huge number: 20 percent of this year's GNP would be a round trillion dollars. It is hard, in these pinched times, to imagine the U.S. government being willing to spend a trillion dollars on anything short of saving the planet, if that. Yet that was the price we paid.

There are two truths about the output gap and the war on inflation that need to be emphasized, because many people would like to deny them. First, the gap was not an accident but a deliberate policy. Second, that policy was bipartisan: Democrats and Republicans share the blame and the credit equally.

First, the deliberateness: The decline in output relative to capacity from 1979 to 1982 was the direct result of a tight money

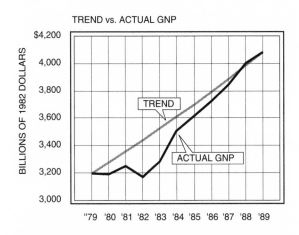

Figure 13
In the 1980s the United States followed a deliberate policy of reducing output relative to its trend, in order to reduce inflation. The cumulative "output gap," which represents the cost of our limited victory over inflation, amounted to more than 20 percent of a year's GNP.

policy instituted by the Federal Reserve aimed expressly at controlling inflation by creating slack in the economy. Of course not every twist and turn was planned. There was a brief, undesired recovery in 1981, to which the Fed overreacted, precipitating an excessively deep recession. But in the end the Federal Reserve got pretty much what it wanted. Using the old-fashioned, painful, but undeniably effective medicine of recession, it brought inflation under control.

Second, the bipartisanship: The policies that produced the output gap began in 1979, under Jimmy Carter, with support from both parties. In the face of near panic over rising inflation, Carter appointed a stern central banker, Paul Volcker, as Chairman of the Federal Reserve Board, and gave him a free hand to do what was necessary. The Reagan administration occasionally sniped at Volcker, but it too basically left him to do as he thought best. Democrats would like to blame the huge cost of the war on inflation on the Republicans; Republicans would like to blame the Democrats for the slump from 1979 to 1982 and take credit for the subsequent recovery. Neither party has a case.

In the end, of course, the war on inflation worked massively to the Republican party's benefit. The pain of rapidly rising unemployment came partly under Carter, and the rest came early enough in the Reagan era to be almost entirely forgotten by now. Meanwhile, the inevitable subsequent recovery of output and the lower rate of inflation helped lend a golden glow to the remaining Reagan years. This political windfall, however, reflected neither wisdom nor Machiavellianism on the part of the governing party, just luck.

What now?

The war on inflation did not end with a complete victory. Inflation has by no means been eliminated, and indeed during the late 1980s it crept up again, before falling in the 1990-92 recession. Will there be a second war on inflation to establish full price stability?

Some people think that there should be. The reason is not that the costs of current inflation are high—even foes of inflation know that they are not. It is that if we relax about inflation it will tend to creep up, and the whole struggle will have to be repeated. For example, Herbert Stein, who dismisses the trade deficit as a "nonproblem," declares inflation to be a real problem. Why? Because "if we . . . relax anti-inflation efforts now, what has been an inflation rate of 4 percent accepted on the assumption that someday we would start to get it down to zero will become a rate of 5 percent accepted on the same assumption and then 6 percent . . . Someday we will have to devote ourselves to getting the rate down, and the longer we wait, and the higher the rate we start from, the more difficult and costly that will be."

On the other hand, there are economists who argue that fear of inflation, rather than inflation itself, is the real problem. Robert Eisner, a liberal economist at Northwestern University, says: "Obsessions about inflation are major obstacles, more inexcusable when the overall price level is almost stable and serious inflation clouds exist only in the minds of those for whom these are perennial fears."

Views like Stein's carried immense moral authority in the late 1980s. In an era when conservative economic principles command more respect than they had for half a century, and with the memories of double-digit inflation still fairly fresh, few policymakers would declare publicly a willingness to tolerate inflation indefinitely. Officially, the Federal Reserve and the Bush administration agreed that the goal should be complete price stability within five years.

That was, however, nearly pure hypocrisy. As the experience of the 1980s shows, reducing the rate of inflation requires high unemployment. Even on an optimistic estimate, to get us from current inflation to price stability over the next five years would mean maintaining an *average* unemployment rate for the next five years of something like 7 percent, not the 5.3 percent that prevailed at the end of the 1980s. The actual U.S. unemployment rate in early 1993 was in fact about 7 percent. But the political system was completely unwilling to live with that rate; instead, the Federal Reserve was under intense pressure to get unemployment down as fast as possible.

So the reality is that moderate inflation, like the trade deficit, has been accepted as a more or less permanent part of the American scene.

III   Policy Problems

Problems are not policies. While the trade deficit and inflation are the principal problems that worry American policymakers, actual policy is concerned with more specific questions—the budget deficit, interest rates, the dollar—that have a bearing on these problems but need to be discussed in their own right.

A description of America's economic policies is inevitably messier than a description of its problems. Policy is rarely a coherent response to perceived problems; more often it represents the outcome of bargains and struggles between groups who not only have disparate interests but also disparate perceptions of reality. It is easy to find examples of policies that seem perverse, or that work at cross-purposes. Yet the six policy issues examined here—health care, the budget deficit, monetary policy, the dollar, trade policy, and Japan—share some underlying themes. Each issue either has, or is thought to have, something to do with the trade deficit. On each issue policy has been constrained by fear of inflation. And on each issue both policymakers and voters have proved willing to accept a level of performance that would have seemed unacceptable 15 or 20 years ago.

Three months into Bill Clinton's presidency, his administration was the target of a strange legal challenge. A number of groups filed suit to demand that the deliberations of the special task force he had convened to develop a new health care policy be opened to the public. Up to that point, the task force had operated in extraordinary secrecy. Interested parties had noticed, however, that federal law requires public access to hearings unless they are restricted to government employees — and the health care task force was being chaired by First Lady Hillary Rodham Clinton, who was technically a private citizen.

The story was a nice illustration of the strangeness of American institutions, but the deeper moral involved the peculiar tensions surrounding the issue of health care. On other issues, the Clinton administration liked nothing better than to make a show of consulting the public; the "town meeting," during which the president took questions from ordinary citizens, was one of his favorite events. Yet health care policy, which affects ordinary people more directly than almost anything else the government does, was being formulated in what some people called a "Manhattan Project" atmosphere, recalling the secret effort that developed the atom bomb.

This was no accident. Health care is an incredibly sensitive subject, which one cannot talk about sensibly without treading on very dangerous emotional and political ground. Previous administrations had preferred to avoid the issue altogether. (The first edition of this book did the same.) Yet the need to do something about health care has become so critical as an *economic* issue that the Clinton administration felt that it had to move quickly to establish a policy. The probably vain hope was that by keeping the discussions secret, the dangers could be avoided.

Why is health care so important? And why is the subject so touchy? The answers go hand in hand.

The health care problem

The trouble with health care is simple: it is eating the U.S. economy alive.

In 1970, public and private spending on health care combined amounted to 7.3 percent of national income. By 1980 the number was 9.1 percent; by 1993 the number was about 13 percent. Rising health care costs were a major reason for the difficulty of controlling the U.S. budget deficit; the costs of providing health insurance to workers were becoming a major burden on the private sector; yet a growing number of Americans were unable to afford health insurance.

At a basic level, there is no puzzle about why health care costs have risen so much. To some extent, the rise in costs is a matter of demography: older people require more health care, and the United States is an aging society. For the most part, however, the story involves the interaction between institutions and technology: an insurance system that can't say no, and a developing medical technology that plays into that weakness.

Start with the basic fact: the great majority of Americans are covered by some form of health insurance. Older people are covered by Medicare; poor people by Medicaid; and most others by some form of private insurance, usually provided by their employers. Insurance doesn't cover everything, but it does cover most big expenses. So when a patient and a doctor discuss a possible test or treatment, they know that a third party will pay the bill.

Now suppose that in this situation there is a test or treatment that is very expensive but that might help a patient. A patient who was paying for his own health care might decide not to proceed, figuring that the money involved would add more to his future quality of life — or, if one wants to be grim about it, to that of his heirs — than the likely benefits of the procedure. But since he doesn't pay for it, he tells his doctor to go ahead. That is, the system does not make any trade-offs between medical gain and economic loss. In the jargon of medical economists, treatment is always pushed to the "flat of the curve": the point at which further expenditure brings no medical benefit, which may be well beyond the point at which a patient whose own money was at stake might decide that the medical benefits were not worth the cost.

This tendency to push treatment to its medical limits, irrespective of cost, has become increasingly expensive over time, thanks to the development of ever more sophisticated medical technologies. Once upon a time, there was only so much that even the rich could spend on medical care: aside from a few surgical procedures and some good advice on public sanitation, as recently as 1940 doctors had little to offer except a consoling bedside manner. Today we have an extraordinary array of possible tests and therapies: CAT scans and MRIs, radiation and chemotherapy, double and triple bypasses. These new techniques save many lives, and make many other lives more comfortable, but they do so at an often enormous price. The flat of the curve moves ever further to the right: we find more and more medically useful ways to spend more and more money on health care.

Does this mean that all Americans receive too much health care? No, because there is a paradox of the system. We will spend virtually unlimited amounts on insured patients, but not everyone is insured. And since insurance becomes increasingly expensive as it is called upon to pay for ever more sophisticated medicine, a growing number of people are unable to afford that insurance — a terrifying position, given the potential costs of medical care. The paradox is that because it tends to make health insurance more costly, improved medical technology actually tends to drive people out of our health care system. It's even possible that medical innovation actually worsens the nation's overall health, because the fancy new treatments do less good than the harm done when people who can no longer afford insurance are priced out of the system.

That is the basic picture of what is wrong with American health care. It seems pretty straightforward. Yet there is a mystery about the problem, which we need to confront before we can talk about possible solutions.

Why can't the system say no?

Let's restate the problem. When an insurer pays the bills, doctors and patients have every incentive to pursue any procedure that may yield a medical benefit, regardless of cost. This in turn makes insurance very expensive, prohibitively so for many people.

But there's a mystery here. Most people are insured privately, not by the government. Why don't private insurers offer "plain vanilla" plans tailored to those who cannot afford the current, expensive plans, or who would prefer to have a little less health care and pay smaller premiums? In principle, one might think, all that an insurer would have to do is impose some limits either on the kinds of procedures a policy will pay for or the maximum amount it will cover. Why doesn't the marketplace just say no to high medical costs?

There seem to be two answers. First is that while we have a lot of doctors in this country, we have even more lawyers. Unless one can spell out in excruciating detail exactly what an insurance plan will or will not pay for — and perhaps even then — it is all too easy to imagine what might happen to an insurance company that tried to offer a policy with more limited coverage than the norm. Suppose that the company refused to pay for some procedure, and then the patient died, or ended up crippled. Wouldn't the insurance company, or even the doctor who decides to limit treatment, be open to a very expensive lawsuit? The costs of medical malpractice insurance are legendary; fear of even more of the same may be one of the main factors making the market for health care ineffective.

There may also be a second, more honorable reason why we can't say no. Medicine is a huge industry, but it is not a business like any other. Doctors and nurses routinely make life-and-death decisions. They have traditionally been governed by an ethical code that expects them to aspire to a higher standard in their professional behavior than simply maximizing profit. While it is easy to be cynical, we all take it as a given that the medical professions will behave better on average than, say, used car dealers.

Now the problem is that an ethos of saving life, of doing the best for the patient — no matter how diluted by the fact that doctors are no more saintly than anyone else — is very difficult to reconcile with a system that explicitly provides radically different levels of care to different people. It is of course true that a billionaire will often manage to get treatments the rest of us don't, but that's very different from imagining a system that explicitly pulls the plug on people with $2,000 policies while keeping the machinery going for those who paid $5,000. A system that allows money pretty explicitly to buy life itself is, rightly, something we find hard even to talk about.

The result of this squeamishness is, however, that all health insurance tends to push toward the same norm, and that this norm is one in which even the most expensive medical technology must be used because it might do some good. Caught between the rapacity of the lawyers and the ethics of the doctors, the market for health care finds itself unable to control costs.

So what's the answer? The debate over health care reform often sounds impossibly technical, filled with complicated ideas expressed in dense jargon. But the essence of the problem — an essence that, as we will see in a moment, is too easily forgotten — is simple: how can we create a set of institutions that can really say no?

Reforming health care

Would-be health care reformers tend to come up with three basic types of idea. The irresponsible ones want something for nothing: they imagine that the problem can be solved by squeezing some set of supposed villains. At the other end are hard-headed types who want the United States to emulate the more or less centralized systems that seem to allow other advanced nations to spend much less on health than we do. Finally, there are the tinkerers, who hope that some clever rearrangement of the medical market can sharply reduce costs.

Looking for villains

When something gets as expensive as health care in the United States, it is a natural reaction to imagine that it is because some-

one—insurers, owners of private hospitals, drug companies — is
profiteering. And without question there are some people and
companies in the health care sector who are overcharging and
exploiting the system. After all, health care is 13 percent of our
economy, directly and indirectly employing at least 14 million
people; without doubt it exhibits the full range of human behavior, from the highest to the lowest.

But can eliminating profiteering be a significant part of the
answer to our health care problems? No: there isn't that much
excess profit, and we probably can't do much about what there
is.

A good illustration of the point came early in 1993, when
there was a brief flurry of accusations of excess profits among
drug companies. There is clear evidence that drug companies
charge more for some of their products in the United States than
they do in Canada, where the national insurance system uses its
bargaining power to hold prices down. There is also some weaker evidence that the pharmaceutical industry earns unusually
high rates of return, even given the riskiness of its business. On
the strength of this evidence, President Clinton made several
speeches lashing out at drug companies. But cooler heads soon
prevailed. After all, even if the excess profits are real — a debat-
able proposition — they add only a few percent to the overall
cost of drugs, which in turn are only about 7 percent of health
costs. And how can we try to control drug prices without discouraging the research and development on which progress
depends? In fact, the president's remarks had an immediate
chilling effect on biotechnology stocks, raising fears that research
and development in that high-technology industry would be
crippled by lack of funds.

It is tempting to try to blame someone for the health care
problem, but looking for villains is not a productive strategy.

Centralized systems

The United States spends more on health care, both in per capita terms and as a share of national income, than any other country. Yet it does not seem to be healthier. Even if one discounts the special problems that come from our high rates of poverty and large underclass, it's hard to see any indication that we are getting much value for our larger investment. What are the other countries doing that we are not?

The most obvious answer is that they have some kind of centralized health care system, in which the government decides how much will be spent — and that such a system is better at saying no than our decentralized system. This may sound paradoxical to people brought up to believe that free markets are always more efficient than governments, but we have already seen that the market for medical care is different from any ordinary market. We have a system in which insurers and doctors cannot say no, either because of fear of legal action or because they are unwilling to violate social norms. Perhaps a government-run plan can restrict access to medical care with less fear of legal action, and can help to establish norms that are somewhat less expensive.

Centralized systems come in two basic variants. European countries typically run medical care as a public service like basic education: hospitals are run by the government, doctors and nurses are government employees. Such systems are forced to take cost into account by the simple force of budget limitations: given a limited amount of money to spend, health care officials must trade off one person's care against another's, which in effect means ruling out procedures that are too expensive. The problem with such a system is, of course, that it limits individual choice, and is subject to all of the usual problems that can afflict a government bureaucracy. The U.S. medical profession has always been bitterly opposed to "socialized medicine," but the system is popular where it exists.

A much milder form of centralized medicine is the "single payer" system that exists in Canada. Canada offers all citizens health insurance, provided by the government; the government sets rates and determines what will be covered, but people are free to choose their own doctors. It seems that this system is also considerably cheaper than the U.S. system, perhaps because the "single payer," the government, can set guidelines on what it will not cover that private insurers in the United States cannot.

A hard-headed approach to health care reform in the United States would be to adopt one of these systems, which do seem to contain costs better than our own. In practice, a national health service on European lines seems to be completely out of bounds for the United States, with its deep distrust of government and powerful private medical interests. A Canadian-style single-payer system is more conceivable, but the most influential advocates of U.S. health care reform think that they can do better with a novel system: managed competition.

Managed competition

The concept of managed competition is the brainchild of the health economist Alain Enthoven, and appears at the time of writing to be the core of the Clinton administration health plan.

Enthoven's idea begins with the observation that a growing number of Americans insure themselves, not with policies that allow them to go to any doctor, but via plans that limit their choices. Many people are insured with Health Maintenance Organizations (HMOs), which maintain their own staffs and require their members to use staff doctors unless they need to be referred to outside specialists. Others are insured with plans that do not maintain a staff, but that do restrict their members to getting care from a "preferred" list of physicians who have agreed to accept the plan's conditions on fees, procedures, and so on. HMOs in particular seem to be able to offer health insurance more cheaply than conventional insurers.

The "managed competition" idea is essentially to organize everyone into large organizations that will either provide health care HMO-style or at least bargain with doctors, drug companies, and so on.

Why might this help? HMOs certainly seem to have some advantages — perhaps because they are simply more efficient, but also perhaps because by joining an HMO an individual effectively gives that organization the right to limit the range of treatment she will receive. That is, one might say that the growth of HMOs is a way of providing something like the "plain vanilla" health insurance that we have seen is very difficult to write into policies.

But there is nothing preventing the growth of HMOs from occurring spontaneously. Why will a deliberate program of pushing people into large health plans improve the situation? And will such a program really deal with the core issue of stopping short of the flat of the curve?

The short answer is that nobody knows. Enthusiastic advocates of managed competition are very influential, but many health-care economists find their enthusiasm a bit puzzling; they can't quite see why rearranging people into big health plans will make much of a difference. The logic of managed competition is not overwhelmingly obvious. And since the system has never been tried, there is no real evidence on how it will work. A major study of the prospects for managed competition by the Congressional Budget Office, released in the spring of 1993, essentially threw up its hands and admitted ignorance: the idea might work, it agreed, but then again it might not.

I find myself among the skeptics. The essential health care problem seems to be one not so much of market structure as of morality. Economic reality requires that we place a price on human life and health, but that's a reality we prefer not to admit, and our unwillingness to face up to that choice explains why costs have exploded. It is hard to see how managed competition can resolve the dilemma. Indeed, one wonders whether the enthusiasm for complex schemes is not just another form of evasion.

The urgency of health care reform

At the time of writing, the Clinton administration had not yet formally released its health care proposal. Initial discussion suggested, however, that the plan would rely primarily on managed competition to control costs. As we have just seen, many experts have little faith in the effectiveness of that solution. In any case, it was highly questionable whether the program would pass a largely hostile Congress.

Nonetheless, health care reform will come sooner or later, for one overwhelming reason. A lot of health care is paid for by the federal government, and health care costs have become a key part of our next policy problem: the budget deficit.

7   The Budget Deficit

It is easy, and perhaps appropriate, to become outraged over the persistence of the federal deficit. Harvard economist Benjamin Friedman, in a book entitled *The Day of Reckoning*, waxes eloquent over "inaction that would have seemed unthinkable not long ago: first the pretense that there was no problem, next the wait for others to make the necessary sacrifices, and finally the complacent conclusion that nothing could be done because nothing would be done." If the apparent acceptance of more or less stagnant living standards is the most striking feature of the diminished expectations Americans have for their economy, the acceptance of a more or less permanent budget deficit is the most spectacular example of the diminished expectations the public has for its elected leaders.

Who's afraid of the deficit?

There are more than two sides to the deficit issue. Indeed, a minimum count is four, since both Democrats and Republicans are divided on the issue. On the Democratic side, one group claims that the deficit is a major problem and must be cured with a tax increase; another group claims that there is no deficit problem and new spending programs should be proposed freely. On the

Republican side, one group proclaims that the deficit is a problem (though not as bad as the Democrats claim) and must be cured by cutting spending; the other claims that there is no problem, although spending should be cut anyway.

Why worry about the federal deficit? In principle, there are two reasons. First, the government's solvency could be in danger. Second, the deficit may have negative side consequences for the economy.

The one thing clear to everyone in the deficit debate is that solvency is not a problem. The U.S. government is nowhere near being unable to pay its bills, because it can easily borrow enough to cover the deficit. Nor is the federal debt growing fast enough to undermine this solvency anytime soon. Although the federal debt grows at $200 billion each year, the economy and hence the federal tax base are also growing. A useful measure of the ultimate solvency of the federal government is the ratio of debt to gross national product. Despite years of unprecedented deficits, this number is not very different from the ratio in other countries, including Japan. Moreover, the ratio has more or less stabilized: Although federal debt grows every year, inflation and the

Figure 14
Despite continuing deficits, the ratio of federal debt to GNP has stabilized at a level not too far out of line with other industrial countries.

growth of the U.S. economy are keeping up with it. Barring an economic crisis that drastically cuts federal revenue or pushes interest rates to unprecedented levels, the federal government will be solvent for the foreseeable future.

So the costs of the federal deficit are milder and more prosaic: It is alleged to drain off an important part of our national saving, leading to a low national savings rate.

Despite periodic attempts by economists to raise public concern about the problem of low national saving, neither the idea of national savings nor the reasons why it may matter have been widely appreciated. So it is worth pausing to consider what national savings are and why we should care.

National savings

The discussion of national savings, like discussion of the budget deficit itself, is a political minefield. National savings are intimately bound up with both the budget deficit and the trade deficit, and therefore with how you read the record of the Reagan administration. That means that almost nobody approaches the subject without some kind of axe to grind, and that almost everyone tries to twist the discussion in a way that reinforces his political agenda. So it's important to start by getting the basics straight.

The first thing to get straight is that the crucial issue is *national* savings—how much the country as a whole saves—not the savings of any particular group inside the country. If I am convinced that national savings are too low, and you can show me that the savings of some particular group, like families, is fairly high, then I will not be appeased. I will simply have to find another culprit.

The second thing to get straight is the definition of saving. Saving means setting aside some portion of your current earnings to provide for the future. There are only two ways that the nation as a whole can save. It can use some of its current income to build more factories, improve its telecommunications, rebuild its streets and bridges, etc. That is, it can add to its stock of productive capital by investing more than enough to replace old capital as it wears out or becomes obsolete. Or it can buy assets from foreigners, either by investing abroad or by paying off debts incurred to foreigners in the past. The national savings rate is therefore measured as the sum of net domestic investment (increases in the capital stock) and net foreign investment (increases in the net claims of the nation on foreigners).

Since the early 1980s domestic investment in the United States has been slightly lower than it was in the past. Meanwhile, America has stopped investing on net abroad and started selling huge quantities of its own assets to foreigners. So the savings of the United States as a whole were much lower in the 1980s than in the past. It's important to keep your eye on that ball. There are economists who will tell you that there really isn't any federal deficit, if you measure it right, or that households are actually saving a lot in indirect ways, and therefore that there really is no problem. Such arguments, however, have nothing to do with the measurement of national savings. They are arguments about why national savings are low. An economist who tells you that there is really less of a budget deficit problem than there seems to be is simply telling you that the causes of low national saving lie elsewhere than in the federal budget. Maybe he's right—but it still remains true that the United States as a whole is saving very much less than it used to.

Figure 15 shows how national savings as a percentage of national income has changed over the past 20 years. Except during the recession years 1974–1975, the national savings rate in the 1970s remained roughly what it had been in the 1950s and 1960s—about 7 percent of income. Then during the 1980s the

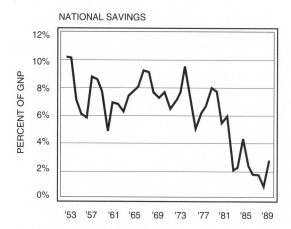

NATIONAL SAVINGS

Figure 15
During the 1970s the United States continued to save about the same fraction of its national income as it had in the 1950s and 1960s. After 1980, however, national savings plunged to the lowest level seen in the postwar period.

rate plunged to the astonishingly low level of 2 percent. Although the savings rate recovered somewhat in 1988 and 1989, it still remains far below its historical level.

The low level of U.S. national savings is particularly striking when we compare our experience with that of other countries. While the United States recently has been saving just 2 to 3 percent of its income, other industrial countries have been saving an average of 10 percent, and Japan has been saving no less than 18 percent.

What are the consequences of low national saving? Recall the definition: national saving is the sum of net domestic and net foreign investment. If savings fall, then domestic investment or foreign investment, or both, must give.

In America's case, the sharp fall in our savings was reflected in slightly lower domestic investment. The most dramatic effect, however, was the decline in our net foreign investment. In the 1970s the United States continued to invest slightly more abroad than foreigners invested here, so our position as a net creditor in the world economy continued to grow. When national savings crashed in the 1980s, however, the United States maintained its rate of investment by becoming a massive net importer of capital—initially by selling foreigners large quantities of bonds, and increasingly by attracting foreigners eager to buy controlling interests in American businesses.

The main consequence of the decline in U.S. saving, then, has been a growing dependence on foreign capital to finance our investment—the flip side of the unprecedented trade deficits of the 1980s.

Why were savings so low in the 1980s? There are two main reasons. First, as everyone knows (but some people choose to deny), the huge federal budget deficit meant that the federal government was engaged in massive dis-saving (or negative saving); that accounts for about half of the decline in saving since the late 1970s. The other big factor was a sharp decline in saving by households; as families reduced their savings and loaded up on consumer credit, the personal savings rate fell to record lows.

Nobody is sure why personal savings fell so much, or whether it will bounce back. Some economists think that personal savings is showing signs of a partial recovery: There was a jump in the personal savings rate after the stock market crash in October 1987, reflecting a new caution on the part of consumers; this new higher rate has persisted. If it continues to rise, then the national savings problem will be somewhat alleviated.

Meanwhile, however, the national savings rate still remains very low by historical standards, bringing with it an inevitable huge trade deficit. Since the trade deficit is widely viewed as a serious problem, why don't we do something to raise savings?

The answer is simple and has become boring through repetition: The only *reliable* way to raise national savings is to eliminate the budget deficit. Although some economists claim that reducing the budget deficit would do little to increase national savings, the reasonable citizen's view is still that a lower budget deficit is the one surefire route to higher national savings. Special incentives, tax reform, and who knows what else might help, or they might not. Eliminating the budget deficit will.

Apologists for the budget deficit

To the extent that there is an orthodox position on the deficit, within both the Republican and Democratic parties, it is the one laid out in the previous section: The budget deficit reduces national saving, helping cause the trade deficit, and should therefore be eliminated. (Where the parties differ is in how.) The deficit, however, has its defenders, on both the left and the right. While the mainstream of both the economics profession and the political community condemns the deficit, self-proclaimed experts have, with vigor and not a little glee, taken on the role of apologists for, and even champions of, the deficit.

The harmless deficit: The view from the left

The defense of the deficit from the left has come from a number of academics and journalists, but the most influential has been Northwestern's Robert Eisner, a past president of the American Economic Association, and an economist with impeccable mainstream credentials. Eisner's argument, at bottom, is that the deficit is a statistical illusion. He rests his case on two points: the effects of inflation in raising the measured deficit, and the difference between the current and capital expenditures of the government.

The inflation point may best be explained by example. Imagine a government with a total debt of a trillion dollars, paying 4 percent interest on the debt, so its total interest bill is $40 billion. Now imagine the same situation, but with an inflation rate of 5 percent—and, because inflation tends to pull up the rate of interest, an interest rate of 9 percent. Interest payments on the debt will then be $90 billion, and the government deficit will be $50 billion larger than in the first example.

But does the government really do the economy any more harm in the second case than in the first? The government itself does not consume any more goods and services. Nor does the larger deficit encourage higher consumption: Owners of government bonds will understand perfectly well that the higher interest rate they receive is offset by the erosion in the value of the bonds by inflation, so they will not feel richer. So the larger deficit in the second case won't lead to higher consumption by either the public or the private sector. But since national saving is simply income less consumption, that means the higher measured deficit will not have a negative effect on national saving.

Eisner calculates that as a result of this inflation illusion, the national deficit of $150 billion is overstated by about $80 billion.

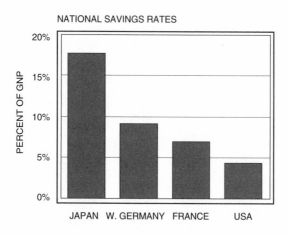

Figure 16
The United States saves far less of its national income than other major industrial countries.

Next he argues that a good chunk of the government's spending is investment, not consumption: building roads; aircraft carriers, and other long-lived assets. One should not count this as part of the government's current expenditure any more than a firm's investment spending is counted against its profits. Thus Eisner concludes that there really isn't any deficit if you measure it right, and we should all relax about the deficit issue. In fact, Eisner and others argue that the really damaging thing is not the deficit but the attack on the deficit, which distorts public priorities.

What's wrong with Eisner's argument? The main problem seems to be that he ignores the context. First, if his arguments are true now, they were even more true fifteen years ago. At the end of the 1970s inflation was much higher than it is now. Furthermore, the attempts to hold down government expenditure in the 1980s have, by most accounts, cut the amount of government *investment* much more than the amount of government *consumption*—if complaints about deteriorating infrastructure are taken seriously, we may even have negative *net* government investment. So a calculation along Eisner's lines leads to the conclusion that under Jimmy Carter the federal government was running a huge surplus! Whether you agree with the measurement is less important than the fact that, however you measure it, the federal government moved sharply *toward* deficit in the 1980s, and thus contributed to the decline in national savings.

And here's where the second criticism of Eisner's argument comes in. Maybe there really isn't any government deficit, but we certainly do have a huge trade deficit. We cannot do much to cut this deficit unless national savings can be raised—and cutting the federal deficit is the only reliable tool we have to do this. So if you are worried about the trade deficit, what difference does it make if Eisner can show that by some measure we don't have a budget deficit?

The harmless deficit: The view from the right

While some on the left deny that there is really a deficit, an influential group of economists on the right argues that it doesn't matter what the deficit is. The leader of this group is Robert Barro of Harvard, whose professional standing is, if anything, even greater than Eisner's. Barro and his followers maintain that as long as the U.S. government is solvent—which it clearly is—the actual size of the deficit is irrelevant.

Barro's argument may be conveyed by the following example. Suppose that the federal government were to announce that it was reducing everyone's taxes this year, that it would cover the revenue loss by selling one-year bonds, and that it would levy a special tax surcharge next year to pay off the bonds. What would be the effect on consumer spending?

Barro says that there would be no effect. Everyone would realize that their higher income this year will be offset by lower income next year, and that they would need to put aside the current tax rebate to pay the higher future taxes. So, according to Barro, just about all of the tax reduction would be saved. The federal deficit would rise, but so would private saving, and national saving would be unaffected.

Generalizing from this example, Barro and his followers contend that changes in tax rates have no effect on national saving. If the government raises taxes now, the reduced government debt will mean lower taxes later, and people will therefore not cut their current consumption.

Does this mean that nothing the government does will affect private spending? No—but what matters is how much the government spends, not how much it collects in taxes. If the government introduces a new spending program, then individuals will realize that this increases the amount of taxes they have to pay—if not now, then later with interest. So they will cut their consumption immediately. The point is not that what the government does is unimportant, but rather that the decision whether to tax now or later, to run a deficit or raise taxes immediately, is basically irrelevant.

Although this view of the deficit is highly abstract, it has two key features that help raise an economic theory to prominence. First, it appeals to the professional instincts of many economists, who always prefer to push the assumption of rational economic behavior as far as possible. Second, it serves a political end: The Barro view, however honestly held by its academic proponents, can be appropriated by apologists for the deficit record of Republicans in the White House. As a result, Barro's views have come to be taken very seriously, both by his colleagues and by intellectually minded conservatives.

Unfortunately, there is nothing in U.S. experience since 1980 that lends empirical support to the Barro view. When the Reagan administration cut taxes without cutting aggregate spending, private savings did not rise—they fell. Moreover, Barro's theory requires that ordinary households be extremely well informed and rational about the future tax implications of current government spending—to a degree that seems quite unlikely. What fraction of the American public knows anything of substance about the federal budget? The notion that ordinary Americans can readily form reasonable estimates of the budget's implications for their tax rates over the rest of their lives strains credulity. In practice, one does not often hear Barro's views expressed directly in Washington's corridors of power. But they do play an important role in maintaining a climate of doubt about whether the budget deficit is really a serious problem.

Reducing the deficit

Despite the deficit's apologists, political orthodoxy still demands that Congress and the administration make a show of doing something about it. What are the options?

In fiscal 1990 the federal government had expenditures of
about $1.2 trillion, with revenues of $980 billion, for an accounting deficit of $123 billion. This number is partly a fraud, thanks
to the desperate accounting expedients used to postpone the
Gramm-Rudman targets; the true deficit was more like $150 bil-
lion. So roughly speaking revenues were only about 85 percent
of expenditures.

Liberals would like to close this gap chiefly by raising taxes,
but are afraid to raise taxes on the middle class. Conservatives
claim that they could eliminate the deficit mainly by cutting
nondefense spending.

The idea that the deficit can be cured largely by cutting nondefense spending is, if it is meant to describe an immediate policy option, nonsense. Figure 17 shows the main reason why. In
essence, the federal government spends the vast bulk of its
money on three things: defense, social insurance programs (primarily Social Security) that mostly benefit the middle class, and
interest on the national debt. Everything else—AIDS research,
education, drug enforcement, antipoverty programs, foreign aid,

COMPOSITION OF FEDERAL EXPENDITURE, 1987

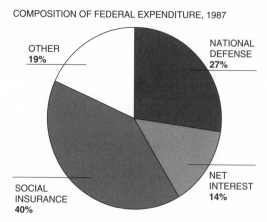

Figure 17
The bulk of federal spending goes for defense, social insurance, and interest on the
federal debt. This makes radical further cuts in total spending nearly impossible.

and the cost of actually running the government—accounts for only 19 percent.

Those who speak about the need to cut government spending usually do not have defense spending or Social Security in mind, nor are they advocating repudiation of the national debt. But even radical cuts in what's left wouldn't eliminate the deficit. In any case, radical cuts are all but impossible. Many of the programs in the "everything else" category have already been sharply curtailed over the past 12 years; meanwhile, demands for new spending, for everything from the war on drugs to aid for Russia and the savings and loan bailout, have been accumulating. So there is no real possibility of closing the gap by cutting spending.[2]

While the public may not know this, everyone in Washington does. What the opponents of tax increases really hope is not to *eliminate* the deficit by *cutting* spending, but to *reduce* it by *restraining* spending. The basic idea is that if the rate of growth of spending can be kept below the rate of growth of the economy, the deficit will gradually fade away without any need either to make sharp spending cuts or to raise tax rates.

The arithmetic of such an approach—dubbed a "flexible freeze" by Michael Boskin, Chairman of George Bush's Council of Economic Advisers—can seem very appealing. Imagine, for a moment, that the U.S. government could hold its total spending constant in real terms for the next five years, while the U.S.

---

2. The sudden collapse of Leninism raised hopes that a "peace dividend" may resolve America's budget woes. Such hopes were exaggerated, for a variety of reasons. First, it is too soon to take events in Europe for granted; surely there are more surprises in store, not all of them pleasant. Second, Europe is not the world. While the end of the Cold War allows a reduction in U.S. forces in Germany, it will be a long time before the United States can comfortably contemplate sharp cuts elsewhere. Third, advocates of a strong defense argue that many cuts of recent years have been penny-wise and pound-foolish; they will press to use the released resources within the Pentagon. Lastly, the enthusiasm over the "peace dividend" already suggests that the dividend will be spent, probably several times over, before any real savings become available.

economy grew at 2.5 percent or more a year and tax revenues grew along with it. The budget deficit would then fall to less than a third of its current ratio to national income, and the ratio of federal debt to GNP would begin to decline. For all intents and purposes the deficit problem would be solved, with no need for either spending cuts or new taxes.

In effect we have already seen the results of a flexible freeze in action. In fiscal 1985 the federal budget deficit was $212 billion, or 5.3 percent of GNP. In fiscal 1988 it was $155 billion, or 3.2 percent of GNP. This deficit reduction was partly due to an increase in the Social Security tax. It was achieved in large part, however, by cutting the rate of growth of spending, scrapping plans for rapid increases in the Pentagon budget, and restraining virtually all other federal programs. The hope of those who oppose tax hikes is that this process can continue, and gradually whittle down the remaining deficit.

Unfortunately, that is unlikely to happen. The reason is that the United States will have a hard time getting away with zero real growth in spending, or anything close to it, in the years ahead. Partly, this is because the responsibilities of the government grow with the economy. As population, employment, and output grow, the country needs more air traffic controllers, more law enforcement, more policing of the environment, etc. So any attempt to avoid spending more means putting an increasing burden on programs that are already stretched to the breaking point. At the same time, efforts to keep the budget numbers artificially low during the Reagan years have left the federal government with an abundance of past due bills.

So the truth is that it's going to be very hard to make rapid progress on reducing the deficit just by restraining spending. Yet for the time being, at least, tax increases large enough to eliminate the deficit are politically out of bounds. That means the budget deficit will remain a more or less permanent fixture on the American economic scene.

A day of reckoning?

If there were any justice in the world, there would be a dramatic end to the deficit story: The adverse consequences of the deficit would become spectacularly apparent in an economic crisis, and the public would rise up and throw the rascals out. But of course there isn't any justice in the world. While there are possibilities of disaster, they don't have to materialize. It is not only possible but probable that budget deficits at more or less the current level will continue for the rest of the century. There will be costs to these deficits, but they may never reach the crisis stage.

Why can America apparently be so irresponsible fiscally yet avoid drastic punishment? At least part of the answer is that even as short-term politics has come to rule the budget, apolitical professionals remain in control of monetary policy.

8   The Embattled Fed

The Federal Reserve sits in the middle of official Washington, three minutes' walk from the State Department, ten minutes from the White House. Yet psychologically it is a world apart. There are no lobbyists crowding the halls, few television crews outside, no "photo opportunities." The senior officials are paid more than their counterparts in the federal bureaucracy; there is no revolving door. Where the top four levels of the rest of the government are filled by short-term political appointees, the Federal Reserve consists of career technocrats top to bottom. It is a serious place, very different in tone from the rest of the U.S. economic policy apparatus. It is also, without question, the most powerful economic institution in the country.

What the Fed does

The Federal Reserve is what the British call a quango—a "quasi-nongovernmental organization." Its complex structure divides power between the federal government and the private banks that are its members, and in effect gives substantial autonomy to a governing board of long-term appointees.

The Fed's power comes from its unique role in controlling the nation's supply of so-called "base money"—the sum total of the currency in the hands of the public and the reserves that banks are legally required to hold to back their deposits. Banks can withdraw their reserves in the form of cash, or deposit cash with the Fed to add to their reserves. But the total quantity of base money cannot be changed except by the Fed's action.

By injecting or withdrawing base money from the system, the Fed has immense influence over the economy. Suppose that the Fed puts more cash in—which it usually does by buying U.S. government debt from a select group of commercial banks. These banks then find themselves with more reserves than they are legally required to hold. They lend out the excess, expanding credit and driving down interest rates. Furthermore, most of the money they lend out ends up being deposited back in the banking system, allowing a second wave of lending, a third, and so on. The result is that the Fed's injection of base money has a multiplier effect, expanding credit throughout the economy. The rise in credit and the fall in interest rates, in turn, stimulates the economy through a variety of channels: housing starts rise, the dollar falls (stimulating exports), business investment rises, consumer credit gets easier. Conversely, if the Federal Reserve withdraws base money from the economy, the process runs in reverse: credit contracts, and the whole economy is restrained.

What is important about the Fed's power to control the economy is how swift and technical its actions can be. Other kinds of economic policy take time and often legislation: tax changes and public works programs take years to craft. The Federal Reserve, meanwhile, can pull the economy out of a recession or (if it makes a mistake) push it into an inflationary boom, cool down an overheated economy or (if it makes the opposite mistake) create a slump—all with nothing more than an instruction to the open market desk in New York to buy or sell.

How should the Fed use this power? The answer its staff has always preferred is "with discretion." That is, they prefer to be left alone, trusted to do the right thing without any specific targets or guidelines. That's the situation they are in now. But they could lose it, and the Fed's struggle to keep its independence is one of the key hidden economic stories in America.

Monetarists, gold bugs, and rational expectations

The Federal Reserve, like so much of the country, was scarred by the Vietnam War, but not in the usual way. The Fed's sin was that when faced with Lyndon Johnson's determination to have both guns and butter, it failed to do its job. Instead of tightening money to keep the economy from overheating, it tried to hold interest rates down. The result was a gradual acceleration of inflation during the second half of the 1960s, from near stable prices to the 4 to 5 percent inflation that passes for stability today.

After a half-hearted attempt to bring down inflation during the first Nixon administration, the Fed did something worse: It allowed a rapid expansion of the economy in 1972–1973, which brought on inflationary pressures from the demand side just as the collapse of an attempt at wage and price controls combined with soaring oil prices to give inflation a huge push from the other side. The result was the worst inflation America had seen since the Civil War. Worse yet, it was difficult to shake off the suspicion that Federal Reserve Board Chairman Arthur Burns took risks with inflation to ensure the reelection of Richard Nixon—a suspicion without any solid evidence to back it, but one that nevertheless haunts the long memories of the Fed.

When inflation took off yet again, in 1979, the Federal Reserve's credibility was badly shaken. The Fed was soon faced with a variety of proposals to strip it of much of its autonomy. What made this effort particularly dangerous, from the Fed's point of view, was the fact that the opponents of an independent Fed had acquired a considerable intellectual cachet.

Since the 1950s, so-called monetarists, led by the University of Chicago's Milton Friedman, have persistently argued that the Federal Reserve, instead of making monetary policy, should follow a simple monetary rule. The essence of the monetarist argument is that discretionary policy on the part of the Fed actually makes the economy less stable, like a driver alternately stomping on the brakes and flooring the gas pedal. Friedman wanted the economy to be put on cruise control. Based on historical studies of the relationship between money and income, Friedman argued that if the Federal Reserve would simply ensure that the money supply grew at a steady rate, say, 4 percent a year, the economy would also grow steadily and without inflation. Between the 1950s and the end of the 1970s, Friedman's arguments gradually took root in educated opinion, changing from scorned iconoclasm to orthodoxy.

After Friedman came the gold bugs, a collection of conservative journalists and politicians whose intellectual clout was supplied by Columbia University's brilliant, eccentric Robert Mundell. The gold bugs argued that even Friedman's rigid targets for the Federal Reserve were not strong enough. A truly sound monetary policy would only come by tying money to an objective outside standard, such as gold.[3] In the 1930s John Maynard Keynes dismissed the monetary role of gold as a "barbarous relic"; yet by the 1980s the call for a return to gold had achieved widespread respectability, capped by a series of gala conferences jointly hosted by Senator Bill Bradley (D-NJ) and Representative Jack Kemp (R-NY).

---

3. A gold standard would be much more extreme than Friedman's rule because it would amount to fixing the quantity of base money. Friedman wanted the Fed to target "monetary aggregates" that included deposits as well as base money; he was aware that even with constant base money large changes in these aggregates could destabilize the economy. For example, at the onset of the Depression the supply of base money in the United States remained constant, but thanks to a banking crisis Friedman's monetary aggregates declined by a third.

Either a full adoption of monetarism or, worse, a revival of the gold standard would take away much of the independence of the Federal Reserve and shift its function from the making of economic policy to narrow technical issues. And that, of course, was the point. Both the monetarists and the gold bugs drew much of their intellectual justification from the influential doctrine of rational expectations. Loosely speaking, this doctrine holds not only that inflation feeds on itself via expectations of future inflation (a common view among economists), but that inflation could be cured quickly and with little pain if the commitment of the monetary authorities not to accommodate inflation could be made credible to the public. Tie the Fed's hands, said the enthusiasts—with rigid monetary targets, or better yet with a gold standard—and we will almost immediately have stable prices with hardly any recession.

The staffers at the Federal Reserve have never been monetarists, and certainly not advocates of a gold standard. They have always believed that their sophisticated judgment would outperform any mechanical rule. In 1979, however, with double-digit inflation, they found it hard to persuade the rest of the country of their competence. The ultimate success of the Fed in persuading the nation that it really does know best was a spectacular example of "judo politics": using the strength of one's opponents to win.

Volcker's victory

In October 1979 the Federal Reserve, under the leadership of Paul Volcker, made a dramatic announcement: Henceforth it would make the targeting of monetary aggregates its chief priority. Publicly, it appeared that monetarism had prevailed.

Three years later the Fed announced that it was abandoning its monetary targets for the year. Since then it has repeatedly done the same, and the targets have attracted steadily less attention. So the Fed, if it was ever monetarist, was monetarist for less than three years.

In retrospect, it seems clear what happened. The Federal Reserve was never monetarist. But it did need to win a major victory against inflation—both for the sake of the economy and to preserve its own treasured independence. It also knew that victory over inflation wouldn't come cheap (rational expectations had few friends at the Fed). The only reliable victory, in its view, would require a deep recession. The question was: How could the Fed persuade the country to swallow such bitter medicine?

Monetarism was the perfect answer. The Fed never said: "We propose to put the country through the worst recession since the 1930s, so that unemployment and excess capacity force the inflation rate down." It simply gave in to its critics and adopted monetary targets. Trying to meet these targets, not incidentally, meant putting the economy through the wringer. But who could criticize the Fed when all it was doing was what its most vociferous critics had been urging all along?

By the late summer of 1982 U.S. inflation was subsiding, but the recession seemed in danger of spiraling out of control. The sudden emergence of the Third World debt crisis raised fears of financial chaos. The result? The Fed cast off its monetarist cloak and returned to an active, discretionary policy. The money spigots were opened, and the economy began a rapid economic recovery. Subsequently the Fed has felt free to fine-tune—reining in the money supply when it fears a resurgence of inflation, pumping it up when the recovery seems to be flagging. In other words, the Fed went back to its traditional position that it knows best, and should not be tied down by someone else's rules.

For those concerned with the long-term independence of the Federal Reserve, the results could not have been better. The limited victory over inflation restored the country's confidence in monetary policy. The pain of the recession was quickly forgotten as the economy recovered. And despite occasional sniping from the White House, the Reagan-Bush administration had little to complain about: The pain came early in Reagan's first term, the recovery came soon enough to fuel a landslide in 1984, and it continued long enough to let Bush coast in four years later.

From a monetarist perspective, Federal Reserve policy after 1982 was nothing short of scandalous. The rate of money growth shifted erratically, sometimes rising to double digits, sometimes becoming negative. For several years after the abandonment of targets, monetarists—Friedman in particular—routinely forecast a disastrous acceleration of inflation and/or a severe recession as a result of monetary instability. Yet the actual result was remarkably smooth sailing, with both the inflation rate and the rate of GNP growth far more stable in the second half of the 1980s than they had been for a long time.

There are still monetarists, but they almost seem like relics now. Milton Friedman's forecasts of doom were at first taken seriously, then ridiculed, then ignored. The gold standard still

Figure 18
Monetary growth was very erratic after the Federal Reserve abandoned its monetarist approach in 1982. Yet output and inflation were remarkably stable.

has friends at the *Wall Street Journal,* but in few other places. At the end of the 1980s the Fed was where it wanted to be: independent, trusted, and not too closely scrutinized.

The 1990–92 recession: A fumble by the Fed

Unfortunately for both the Fed and the country, the institution's reputation for overwhelming competence did not remain intact in the early 1990s. A series of miscalculations by the Fed's Board of Governors allowed the U.S. economy to slide into a painful recession; aside from the toll in failed businesses and lost jobs, this slump threatened once again to undermine the Fed's autonomy.

Economists are still somewhat puzzled by the suddenness of the slump that developed in 1990, in particular by an abrupt decline in consumer confidence. It was almost as if the American public took stock of the 1980s as soon as they were over, found the decade wanting, and decided that the time had come for some austerity. Still, the Federal Reserve has enormously powerful policy instruments and great flexibility in using them. Why didn't it manage to end the recession quickly?

One answer is that during the early stages of the slump the Fed's mind was on other things. In the late 1980s there was considerable agitation by conservative economists and their congressional allies for a U.S. policy aimed not simply at holding the line on inflation but at achieving complete price stability. The Fed wasn't prepared to launch another all-out war on inflation, but it was willing to contemplate some rise in unemployment, especially because many Fed staffers (and many independent economists) believed that the very low unemployment rates of 1989 were somewhat below the NAIRU. One Fed economist remarked to me at about that time that "we can't go out and create a recession, but we can try to take advantage of any little

recessions that come along." This attitude probably made it difficult for the Fed to react quickly as it became increasingly clear
that the developing recession was not a little one at all.

Once the Fed did start trying to stimulate the economy, it
repeatedly overestimated the effectiveness of interest rate cuts,
and was therefore consistently behind the curve as the recession
gained momentum. With the benefit of hindsight, we can see
that some of the usual channels of Fed influence were somewhat
clogged by legacies of the 1980s. Monetary policy works through
an expansion of credit; but many banks, overextended during
the 1980s, were under pressure from regulators to be conservative lenders (see chapter 12). One of the sectors that is usually
most responsive to interest rates is construction of commercial
real estate; but over-optimism had led to a huge oversupply of
offices and shopping malls. The Fed was by no means without
influence—interest rate cuts still worked in stimulating borrowing through the bond market, in encouraging purchases of new
homes, and in many other ways. The point was, however, that as
the recession was spreading the Fed was repeatedly cutting
interest rates too little, too late.

In the end, the usual policies had the usual effects. Output
bottomed out in mid-1991. Initially growth was too slow to keep
unemployment from rising, especially because productivity
grew surprisingly quickly; but an unambiguous recovery was
under way by late 1992.

The fumbles by the Fed, however, threatened its independence, as critics—this time from the left—argued that the central
bank had not done enough to fight unemployment, and worried
that it would undermine the recovery by tightening money too
soon. At the time of writing, the Fed was making obvious efforts
to placate and reassure the new Democratic masters of
Washington that it would not stand in their way—efforts ludi-
crously symbolized when an obviously uncomfortable Alan

Greenspan was photographed seated between the First and Second Ladies in a theater box.

In the end, though, it seems unlikely that the peculiar institution of the Fed will be tampered with. Despite its fumbles, it has almost certainly managed the economy more effectively than one could have expected from any more conventionally political organization.

9   The Dollar

The gyrations of U.S. dollar policy must often seem mysterious to even the most intelligent laypeople. First we liked our dollar strong: In early 1985 Ronald Reagan, in a widely quoted speech, pointed to the strength of the dollar on foreign exchange markets as proof of the success of U.S. economic policies. But soon afterward we wanted it weak: In September 1985 Treasury Secretary James Baker, in a widely praised move, convened a meeting at the Plaza Hotel in New York at which the major industrial countries agreed to try to drive the dollar down. Then we changed our minds again: The same countries agreed in another meeting, at the Louvre in February 1987, to stabilize exchange rates—which initially meant holding the dollar up.

Apparently, this effort was too successful: Through much of 1989 the Japanese and the Europeans tried without much success to keep the dollar from rising.

Through all these policy zigs and zags the economic experts have offered a running commentary that is even more confusing than usual, with some economists insisting that the dollar is grossly undervalued even as others argue that it is greatly overvalued. What's all this about?

To make sense of the dollar issue, it is necessary to ask what purpose dollar policy is supposed to serve. The answer is that we are trying to use dollar policy to help reduce our trade deficit. The reason there is so much confusion is that there are three unsettled points. First, are we really serious about reducing our trade deficit? Second, if we are, does trying to manage the dollar help? And third, if a managed dollar helps, where should it go?

Are we serious about reducing the trade deficit?

Arguably the United States has no real interest in getting its trade deficit down. As previously noted, our trade deficit does not really cost us jobs; the only certain harm it does is to increase our foreign debt, saddling future generations with the burden of paying our current bills. However, unless we are prepared to raise domestic saving, which basically means a sizable cut in the budget deficit, any attempt to reduce the trade deficit will come at the expense of higher interest rates and lower investment. There is a good case to be made that the United States should worry about savings, but not about the trade deficit.

Now we cannot run trade deficits forever. But, as Herbert Stein has pointed out, the nice thing about things that cannot go on forever is that they won't. Why not, then, simply rely on the market? A trade deficit poses no problem so long as foreign investors are willing to finance it, and it will correct itself as soon as they are not. So why have an active government policy of reducing the trade gap?

There are three standard arguments for such a policy, two economic and one political.

First, while trade deficits do always correct themselves, history suggests that the process is not always gentle. To take the most worrisome example, through the 1970s and the early 1980s Latin America ran persistent large deficits, which foreign investors seemed happy to finance. As late as 1981 the consensus was that Latin America could continue to borrow extensively for years to come. Yet in less than a year there was a collapse of financing that forced Latin American economies to cut imports by as much as two-thirds, plunging the region into a deep slump from which it still has not fully emerged. With the benefit of hindsight, it is clear that the governments of Latin America should have worried about their trade deficits, and taken steps to bring them down, while foreign financing was still easy, instead of waiting for the crunch.

The second argument, related to the first, is that reducing the trade deficit takes time. Firms do not change suppliers, or consumers shift to different products, overnight. Turning a trade deficit around often means building new capacity, new distribution networks, and so on. The U.S. experience with the declining dollar is illustrative. The dollar began declining in early 1985, yet the trade deficit actually continued to rise until mid-1987. If we think that the trade deficit will or should begin to shrink sometime in the future, even if the event is two or three years off, it is a good idea to start giving firms incentives to increase exports and reduce imports now. Of course, if the market could be counted on to be farsighted, if exchange rates and the investment plans of firms could be counted on to reflect a careful appreciation of long-term prospects, no special policy would be needed here. But nothing in recent experience suggests that markets are particularly farsighted.

Third, dollar politics cannot be separated from trade politics. The trade deficit feeds protectionist pressures in the United States. Unless that deficit can be seen to be declining, it may be impossible for an administration, no matter how free trade–minded, to contain those pressures.

So there is a case for having a policy of getting the trade deficit down. It is not a watertight case—reasonable people can and do argue that the trade deficit should not be a public policy concern—but as a practical matter the U.S. government does worry about the trade deficit and hopes to see it decline.

Hopes are not, of course, the same as actions. The orthodox recipe for reducing a trade deficit is to combine currency depreciation with fiscal austerity. The United States has been willing to try the first, but not the second. So we can legitimately ask whether it makes sense to try to do anything about the dollar until there are clear signs that a budget solution is in sight.

The answer is a definite maybe. National savings may be on the rise—even without dramatic action on the budget. That makes room for some reduction in the trade deficit.

Furthermore, there is another piece that should be brought into the picture: Most estimates suggest that at the current level of the dollar the U.S. trade position will actually *worsen* substantially over the next few years. So we may need to do something just to keep the trade deficit from rising.[4]

Lastly, given the political dangers arising from protectionism, it makes some sense to take risks in order to keep the trade deficit down. The efforts to bring down the dollar after 1985 were condemned by all the predictable voices as dangerously inflationary; in retrospect things turned out just fine.[5]

Yet, as noted in the last chapter, there are serious risks in putting too much emphasis on trade deficit reduction. In fact, the case for getting the trade deficit down is much weaker than the case for using a lower dollar to get there.

---

4. The U.S. trade deficit could be expected to widen as the economy recovered. In 1992 the current account deficit was $60 billion, or only 1 percent of national income; but the economy was operating well below capacity, probably at least 5 percent below its potential output. As the economy recovered, it would spend more on imports; given the historical relationship between output and imports, a rough estimate would be that at more or less full employment the U.S. current account deficit would have been close to 2.5 percent of GDP.

5. As always, there are voices on the other side. The same Robert Eisner who argues that there really isn't any federal budget deficit is harshly critical of the Fed for "guarding excessively against inflation" and keeping the dollar strong. Eisner would have an all-out push to drive the dollar down.

Dollar policy

The principal tool that the United States has to influence its trade balance is the value of the dollar on foreign exchange markets. The conventional wisdom holds that if the dollar's price in terms of foreign currencies can be reduced, U.S. goods will become more competitive on world markets, and the trade deficit will fall. That is why we had a deliberate policy of reducing the value of the dollar in 1985 and 1986, why the major economies tried to hold the dollar down in 1989, and why many economists and policymakers argue that the dollar needs to fall still lower.

As in so many areas of economics, this conventional wisdom is under attack from both right and left. On both sides, it is alleged that reducing the foreign exchange value of the dollar is ineffective at reducing the trade deficit, and harmful in other ways.

The attack from the right has, as usual, more powerful support—notably the *Wall Street Journal*. Conservative advocates of a gold standard, which would preclude any devaluation of the dollar, are naturally opposed to the idea that changing exchange rates can do any good. They therefore are attracted to the arguments of such people as Stanford's Ronald McKinnon, Columbia's Robert Mundell, and supply-side enthusiast Jude Wanniski, who claim that:

(1) the trade deficit is determined by the balance between savings and investment, not the value of the dollar, so depreciating the dollar can't help reduce it;

(2) depreciating the dollar leads to U.S. inflation, which will wipe out any apparent gains in the cost competitiveness of American industry.

Like most appealing but wrong arguments, this one starts from some valid observations. The trade deficit *does* ultimately depend on the balance between savings and investment, and depreciating the dollar *can* lead to inflation that wipes out competitive gains. But since the exchange rate plays such a crucial role in translating changes in national savings or investment demand into changes in the trade deficit, it is odd to suppose that changing the price of U.S. goods relative to foreign by 25 or 50 percent somehow doesn't affect what we buy and sell.

As for the argument that dollar depreciation just produces inflation, not a real improvement in competitiveness, this merely shows the perennial popularity of ideology over evidence. From 1985 to 1987, the dollar fell almost 50 percent against the West German mark and the Japanese yen. Did U.S. prices double? Was there even a sharp acceleration in U.S. inflation? No. In fact, the dollar's fall was reflected almost exactly one-for-one in a change in the *real* exchange rate—the price of U.S. goods and services relative to those in other countries.

The attack from the left focuses on a different issue: foreign trade policy. Critics of dollar depreciation such as journalist Robert Kuttner argue that it is pointless to try to reduce the trade

Figure 19
The decline of the dollar was reflected almost one-for-one in a reduction of the prices of U.S. goods and services relative to those of foreigners.

deficit by reducing the value of the dollar. Why? Because our foreign competitors simply won't allow American goods in.

Again, the evidence on the whole contradicts this view. If the basic problem is that foreign markets are closed to the United States, here's what we would expect to see when the dollar falls: U.S. imports would fall because U.S. consumers would switch to cheaper domestic products; but U.S. exports would not rise because foreigners would not admit our goods. In fact, what happened when the dollar fell was just the opposite. U.S. exports grew very rapidly; if the trade balance didn't improve as much as we would like, it was because U.S. imports also kept growing. This suggests that the problem is not so much America's lack of access to foreign markets as its taste for foreign imports. (There is a caveat to all of this. We do have a problem exporting to one country: Japan. For the problem of reducing the U.S. trade deficit, this is only a partial obstacle, since Japan is only part of the world. But for American trade policy, Japan is the central problem, as we shall see.)

Can driving the dollar down help reduce the trade deficit? On this issue the conventional wisdom wins, hands down: Yes, it can.

How far is down?

The decline of the dollar from 1985 to 1987 had an unmistakable impact on the U.S. trade position. From 1981 to 1986, the volume of U.S. imports rose inexorably, while U.S. exports stagnated. After 1986, U.S. exports surged while import growth slowed. Indeed, from 1987 to 1991 exports from the United States actually grew faster than those from any other major industrial country.

Yet the results of the dollar's decline remained somewhat disappointing. After all, in 1980 the United States actually exported more goods and services than it exported. By 1992 just about all of the dollar's rise had been eliminated. Against some currencies, including both the mark and the yen, the dollar reached historic lows. Yet the United States continues to run a significant current account deficit: the 1992 deficit was $60 billion, and if the U.S. economy had not been so depressed, it might well have been as high as $150 billion.

There are two obvious, related questions here: Why didn't the fall in the dollar do more? And how far does the dollar have to fall?

The most important answer is probably the obvious one: The United States is just not as competitive as it used to be. Once upon a time we could sell our goods on world markets, even with a very strong dollar, because of our technical superiority. America made things nobody else could, and it produced goods known for their quality. Today the United States often lags behind Japan and even Western Europe in technology, and at least in consumer goods we have developed an impressive reputation for shoddiness. So even though the dollar is back where it

RATES OF EXPORT AND IMPORT GROWTH

Figure 20
The falling dollar sparked a U.S. export boom, but imports kept on rising, so the trade deficit did not fall as much as hoped.

used to be, the United States is not able to sell as much on world markets as it was.

This is not a new development. The 1980 dollar was much weaker than the 1970 dollar, yet the U.S. trade position in 1980 was about the same as it was in 1970. In other words, although the United States was fairly successful at selling its goods on world markets throughout the 1970s, it was able to do so only because of a dollar that weakened steadily against foreign currencies. Apparently this trend continued through the 1980s. The falling dollar has been chasing a moving target.

Figure 21 shows a suggestive picture that may help explain the persistence of the U.S. trade deficit. It shows the actual course of the dollar since 1970, as well as a trend line that tracks the change in the dollar from 1970 to 1980 and then continues downward at the same rate through the 1980s. What the picture reveals is that, despite the decline in the dollar since 1985, the dollar has been much stronger relative to its long-run downward trend in the 1980s than it was in the 1970s. So in a way we

Figure 21
The dollar apparently needs to fall steadily over time if the United States is to balance its trade.

should not be surprised to find that the decline in the dollar has not done more to reduce the trade deficit.

But how far is down? Figure 21 suggests that the dollar would have to fall about 25 percent from its current level to be back on the trend line. This estimate is roughly in line with typical econometric estimates of the fall in the dollar that would be necessary to eliminate the US current account deficit once the economy is back to more or less full employment. (A 20 percent fall in the dollar would mean an exchange rate of a bit less than 100 yen to the dollar, compared with a rate of 120 in early 1993.) The fact that we get about the same number from two different calculations doesn't mean that it is right, but it suggests that the answer to the question "How far is down?" is "A pretty long way."

Should the dollar be driven down?

To eliminate the U.S. trade deficit, or even to reduce it to modest proportions, probably requires driving the dollar down substantially from its current level. Yet the recent trend has actually been one of a rising dollar, opposed but not prevented by official action. Why don't we make dollar depreciation a priority?

One good reason has already been pointed out. We aren't actually serious about getting the trade deficit down—at least not yet. The textbook recipe for curing a trade deficit calls for a lower dollar combined with a lower budget deficit. If we have no intention of actually cutting the deficit any time soon, then it's too soon to seek a lower dollar.

Other, less good reasons have also been mentioned: right-wing claims that a lower dollar would be both ineffective and inflationary, and left-wing charges that dollar depreciation is pointless in the face of foreign barriers to American products at any price.

There is one additional argument—associated with trade poli-cy hard-liners like Clyde Prestowitz and Robert Kuttner—which we are likely to hear more of in the next few years. It goes like this: Depreciating the dollar is a bad way to reduce the trade deficit because it amounts to meeting international competition by cutting American wages, thus lowering the living standards of American workers. Kuttner, in particular, has derided econo-mists who want to "devalue the dollar to the point where we are a poor country."

But if a lower dollar imposes too great a cost on living standards, what is the alternative? The answer of Kuttner, Prestowitz, and others is to rely on trade policy. Instead of low-ering the dollar, they say, the United States should get tough and demand that foreign nations open their markets to U.S. goods. That way, the trade deficit can come down without the need to cut U.S. wages.

This is an appealing argument, and not without some merit. It is also quite misleading, in two ways. First, it makes dollar depreciation sound much worse than it is. When the dollar falls by, say, 30 percent against the yen and the mark, a 30 percent reduction does occur in U.S. wages relative to those in Germany and Japan. But this is not the same as saying that U.S. real wages fall by 30 percent: They probably fall by no more than 1.5 per-cent. Why? Because even now most of the goods and services we consume are made at home, and a fairly large part of our imports tend to be priced in dollars, too. Second, the idea that the United States can realistically expect to get trade concessions from other countries that would be an adequate substitute for a lower dollar is wishful thinking.

Yet the trade deficit, and the frustrations of dollar policy, inevitably put the alternative of protectionism on the table. And if the trade deficit grows, as seems likely, then protectionism is sure to become more and more appealing to many politicians.

10   Free Trade and Protectionism

When future historians list the achievements of the United States during the 45 or so years that it acted as the undisputed leader of the world's democracies, special emphasis is sure to be given to the creation of a relatively free and open world trading system. From about 1950 until the early 1970s, protectionist barriers to world trade came down steadily, and world trade grew rapidly. Nearly everyone thinks that this growth in trade was a good thing.

Yet there are now powerful forces in the United States working against free trade. Much of the argument for protectionism represents sheer interest-group politics: It comes from well-organized groups that are losing out to foreign competition and want protection, never mind the national interest. Yet not all the opponents of free trade are hired guns (and not all its supporters are disinterested, either). It's important to look at both the political sources of protectionism and its intellectual foundations.

The politics of protectionism

The basic rule of trade politics is that producers count more than consumers. The benefits of a trade restriction are usually concentrated on a relatively small, well-organized, and well-informed group of producers, while its costs are usually spread thinly over a large diffuse group of consumers. As a result, the beneficiaries of a trade restriction are usually much more effective politically than its victims.

The classic case in the United States is the import quota on sugar, which benefits a handful of domestic producers at a typical annual cost to consumers of $1 billion a year. This quota goes unchallenged, because the $5 average annual cost per person is so small that probably not one voter in 200 even knows that the import restriction exists.

But if consumers offer no effective opposition to protection, why is U.S. trade relatively free? Because *exporters* advocate free trade. Exporters by definition want access to foreign markets and are as well organized as import-competing producers. For the past 45 years the United States and other advanced countries have used this fact to provide a framework for maintaining relatively free trade. Trade policies are not set unilaterally; they are negotiated between countries.[6] In these negotiations, U.S. import restrictions must be traded off against the import restrictions of other countries, so that U.S. exporters become a powerful voice urging us to accept imports from other countries if they will accept our exports in return.

The source of new protectionist pressure is now obvious. When the United States is running a huge trade deficit, the exporters who want open markets are outnumbered by the import-competing groups who want protection. If in 1980 you had told trade specialists that America would run trade deficits of more than $100 billion for seven years on end, they would surely have predicted more, not less, protection than we have seen.

---

6. The framework for these negotiations is usually the celebrated General Agreement on Tariffs and Trade, or GATT. GATT negotiations take place in a series of "rounds," of which the current, originally scheduled to be concluded in late 1990, was still unfinished at the time of writing.

The relatively mild protectionist reaction so far is a tribute to the strength of free-trade ideology in the United States. The question is how long this can last. It may be useful to think of the United States as having a "protectionist overhang": a back-log of potential pro-tectionist reaction barely held in check. Fear of this reaction is one of the main reasons for worrying about the trade deficit. If the trade deficit continues, sooner or later the persistent demands for more protection are likely to become irresistible.

But what would be wrong with that? Is protectionism really a fate to be greatly feared?

The (limited) evils of protectionism

Although most policymakers in Washington are convinced that protectionism is a bad thing, few of them have any clear idea why. In popular arguments against protectionism, the usual warning is that protectionism threatens our jobs—the Smoot-Hawley tariff of 1931, we are told, caused the Depression, and history can repeat itself.

Although protectionism *is* usually a bad thing, it is worth pointing out that it isn't as bad as all that. Protectionism does not cost our economy jobs, any more than the trade deficit does: U.S. employment is essentially determined by supply, not demand. The claim that protectionism caused the Depression is nonsense; the claim that future protectionism will lead to a repeat performance is equally nonsensical.

The real harm done by protectionism is much more modest and mundane: It reduces the efficiency of the world economy. To the extent that countries limit each other's exports, they block the mutually beneficial process by which nations specialize in producing goods for which their knowledge and resources are particularly well fitted. They also fragment markets, preventing firms and industries from realizing economies of scale. A protectionist country is usually less productive and thus poorer than it would have been under free trade; a protectionist world economy almost always so (see the accompanying box).

Just how expensive is protectionism? The answer is a little embarrassing, because standard estimates of the costs of protection are actually very low. America is a case in point. While much U.S. trade takes place with few obstacles, we have several major protectionist measures, restricting imports of autos, steel, and textiles in particular. The combined costs of these major restrictions to the U.S. economy, however, are usually estimated at less than three-quarters of 1 percent of U.S. national income. Most of this loss, furthermore, comes from the fact that the import restrictions, in effect, form foreign producers into cartels that charge higher prices to U.S. consumers. So most of the U.S. losses are matched by higher foreign profits. From the point of view of the world as a whole, the negative effects of U.S. import restrictions on efficiency are therefore much smaller—around one-quarter of 1 percent of U.S. GNP.

Other countries are more protectionist than the United States, and in some Third World nations wildly inefficient protectionist policies have caused major economic losses. Among advanced countries, however, protectionism at current levels is not a first-class issue. Without a doubt the major industrial nations suffer more, in economic terms, from unglamorous problems like avoidable traffic congestion and unnecessary waste in defense contracting than they do from protectionism. To take the most extreme example, the cost to taxpayers of the savings and loan bailout alone will be at least five times as large as the annual cost to U.S. consumers of all U.S. import restrictions.

If the costs of protectionism are so mild, why does the defense of free trade loom so large on the public agenda? Symbolism and politics. Ideologically, free trade is an important touchstone for

The costs of trade conflict

A hypothetical scenario may be useful for understanding what the costs of protection are, and why they are more modest than many people seem to think.

Let's imagine that most of the world's market economies were to group themselves into three trading blocs—one centered on the United States, one centered on the European Economic Community, and one centered on Japan. And let's suppose that each of these trading blocs becomes highly protectionist, imposing a tariff against goods from outside the bloc of 100 percent, which we suppose leads to a fall in imports of 50 percent.

So we are imagining a trade war that cuts the volume of world trade in half. What would be the costs of this trade war?

One immediate response would be that each bloc would lose jobs in the industries that formerly exported to the others. This is true; but each bloc would correspondingly gain a roughly equal number of jobs producing goods it formerly exported. There is no reason to expect that even such a major fragmentation of the world market would cause extra unemployment.

The cost would come instead from reduced efficiency. Each bloc would produce goods for itself that it could have imported more cheaply. With a 100 percent tariff, some goods would be produced domestically even though they could have been imported at half the price. For these goods there is thus a waste of resources equal to the value of the original imports.

But this would be true only of goods that would have been imported in the absence of tariffs, and even then 100 percent represents a maximum estimate. Our three hypothetical trading blocs would, however, import only about 10 percent of the goods and services they use from abroad even under free trade.

A trade war that cut international trade in half, and which caused an *average* cost of wasted resources for the displaced production of, say, 50 percent, would therefore cost the world economy only 2.5 percent of its income (50 percent x 5 percent = 2.5 percent).

This is not a trivial sum—but it is a long way from a Depression. (It is roughly the cost of a 1 percent increase in the unemployment rate.) And it is the result of an extreme scenario, in which protectionism has a devastating effect on world trade.

If the trade conflict were milder, the costs would be much less. Suppose that the tariff rates were only 50 percent, leading to a 30 percent fall in world trade. Then 3 percent of the goods originally used would be replaced with domestic substitutes, costing at most 50 percent more. If the typical domestic substitute costs 25 percent more, then the cost of the trade conflict is 0.75 percent of world income (25 percent x 3 percent = 0.75 percent).

advocates of free-market economics. As Paul Samuelson once pointed out, comparative advantage is one of the few ideas in economics that is true without being obvious. Politically, free trade is important as a counterweight to crude economic nationalism. So free trade has passionate defenders in a way that other, equally worthy causes—such as economically efficient environmental regulation—do not.

Even if protectionism isn't the most terrible thing in the world, however, it is still a bad thing. Or is it? While the great weight of educated opinion still condemns protection, there are some arguments in its favor.

Protection and the trade deficit

Arguments in favor of protection come in two basic forms. One argument wants the United States to use the *threat* of protection to extract concessions from foreign countries; those who use this argument are not advocating protection per se, but they are willing to use protection as a bargaining threat—a bluff that they are presumably willing to see carried out, at least occasionally. The other argument takes protection to be an intrinsically good thing, at least in some cases.

The bargaining argument for protection is usually stated in the context of the problem of lowering the trade deficit. The United States needs to reduce its trade deficit, say the advocates of this position; but driving down the dollar is ineffective because of foreign trade barriers and reduces American living standards. So let's instead expand our exports by threatening to limit our imports: This will force foreigners to open their markets and allow us to reduce the trade deficit without the need for a much lower dollar.

The main problem with this proposal is that it won't work. It is just not realistic to expect increased access to foreign markets to make more than a minor contribution to reducing the U.S. trade deficit, with or without U.S. pressure. The reasons are both economic and political.

First, the economics. When we talk about removing foreign barriers to U.S. exports, what do we mean? Despite the rhetoric, there are only a few major legislated foreign programs that have a large identifiable impact on U.S. exports; most of these are in the agricultural area. If Japan opened its rice market, or Europe canceled its agricultural support programs, this would help U.S. exports, but it would fall far short of curing our trade deficit. [7]

Meanwhile, there are political realities. U.S. pressure is simply not going to force radical changes in economic policy abroad. The major barriers to American exports are programs, like Europe's agricultural policy, with powerful domestic constituencies. American pressure may induce marginal changes in these programs, but it is a fantasy to imagine that by getting tough we can force other countries to abandon them. The U.S. economy is no bigger than Europe's, and not much bigger than Japan's. Politicians in other countries answer primarily to domestic interests, just as ours do. We cannot expect to bully Europe or Japan into doing things our way any more than they could expect to do the same to us.

Given these economic and political realities, the proposal to use the threat of protection to solve the trade deficit will, in practice, inevitably degenerate into the implementation of that threat. To say that you favor using potential import quotas as a way to spur U.S. exports is, in the end, disingenuous: The result will almost always be fewer imports rather than more exports.

Indeed, however much they may talk about spurring exports, the advocates of a tougher trade policy seem much more

---

7. There is a special issue of access to the Japanese market, which is less of a matter of identifiable restrictions than of the whole structure of Japan's economy; we'll come back to that in the next chapter. But even if something could be done to remove the "structural impediments" to imports in Japan, it would not make a large difference to U.S. exports.

interested in limiting imports. Robert Kuttner's own manifesto
on trade policy, which advocates a broad system of "managed
trade," takes as its model the Multi-Fiber Arrangement: an international treaty that purely and simply restricts trade in textiles
and apparel. That is, in the end he views protectionism not as a
bargaining chip but as a permanent policy.

But what's so bad about that? We have just seen that the conventionally measured costs of protection are not very large. And
there are intellectually respectable arguments suggesting that
protection may, in some cases, actually be beneficial.

The economic case for protection

Economic theories matter, though not necessarily in the ways
that their creators might have wished. In the 1970s public
finance economists, Martin Feldstein prominent among them,
worked hard to persuade the economics profession that flaws in
the tax system distort incentives and retard U.S. economic
growth. The result was to help create a climate of opinion in
which supply-side economists could advocate radical tax cuts,
leading to the massive budget deficits that Feldstein took the
lead in denouncing. In the late 1970s and early 1980s a group of
international economists—myself among them—similarly
worked to persuade the economics profession that the principles
of international trade needed to be rethought. This rethinking of
international trade has won tenure and academic prestige for its
leaders. But an unintended by-product of the effort has been to
lend some new intellectual respectability to protectionism.[8]

8. The "new international economics" is generally associated with several people:
Princeton's Avinash Dixit, Tel Aviv's Elhanan Helpman, James Brander and Barbara
Spencer of the University of British Columbia, and myself. The most widely read
summary of the new ideas is a book I edited, *Strategic Trade Policy and the New
International Economics* (MIT Press, 1986); an excellent summary of the policy impli-
cations is *Who's Bashing Whom?* (Institute for International Economics, 1992) by
Laura D'Andrea Tyson, who is now Bill Clinton's chief economic adviser.

Traditional international economics attributes international trade to underlying differences among countries. Australia exports wool because its lands are well suited to sheep grazing, Thailand exports labor-intensive manufactures because of its abundance of labor, and so on. The new international economics, while not denying the importance of this traditional view, adds that much international trade also reflects national advantages that are created by historical circumstance, and that then persist or grow because of other advantages to large scale either in development or production. For example, the development effort required to launch a new passenger jet aircraft is so large that the world market will support only one or two profitable firms. Once the United States had a head start in producing aircraft, its position as the world's leading exporter became self-reinforcing. So if you want to explain why the U.S. exports aircraft, you should not look for underlying aspects of the U.S. economy; you should study the historical circumstances that gave the United States a head start in the industry.

Why does this provide a potential justification for protectionism? Because if the pattern of international trade and specialization largely reflects historical circumstances rather than underlying national strengths, then government policies can *in principle* shape this pattern to benefit their domestic economies. As journalist James Fallows put it in a recent plea for a more aggressive U.S. trade policy, "Countries that try to promote higher-value, higher-tech industries will eventually have more of them than countries that don't."

Which industries should a country try to promote? One criterion is the potential for technological spillovers. Suppose that you believe that whichever country develops a high-definition television (HDTV) industry will find that its other industries, such as computers and semiconductors, gain an edge over their foreign competitors from their close contact with HDTV

producers. Then it might be worth developing an HDTV sector—even if it requires a continuing subsidy due to costs that are
persistently above those of foreign imports. This is an old argument, but it becomes much more attractive if the new theory is
right, because the new theory suggests that the need for subsidy
may be only temporary: Because comparative advantage is often
created, not given, a temporary subsidy can lead to a permanent
industry.

Another potential criterion for industry targeting has a sexy
name: "strategic trade policy" (a term that is also loosely used to
refer to the technological argument). A hypothetical example
may convey its essence. Imagine that there is some good that
could be developed and sold either by an American or a
European firm. If either firm developed the product alone, it
could earn large profits; however, the development costs are
large enough that if both firms tried to enter the market, both
would lose money. Which firm will actually enter? The answer
may be determined by government intervention. If European
governments subsidize their firm, or make it clear that it will
have a protected domestic market, they may ensure that their
firm enters while deterring the U.S. firm—and thereby also
ensure that Europe, not America, gets the monopoly profits.

The strategic trade policy story (using the term to refer to both
arguments) is not, at base, an argument for protectionism per se.
It is really an argument for a limited government industrial policy consisting of carefully targeted subsidies, not for tariffs and
import quotas. Yet it provides advocates of protectionism with a
new intellectual gloss to justify their position, and it has been
picked up enthusiastically by advocates of "managed trade" like
Clyde Prestowitz and Robert Kuttner. If they do not argue that
the United States should adopt a strategic trade policy, they at
least claim that other countries—primarily Japan—have already
done so, and that the United States needs to respond. As Kuttner

puts it, "the New View radically alters the context of debate, for it removes the premise that nations such as Japan which practice strategic trade could not, by definition, be improving their welfare." There is a strong temptation for both politicians and intellectuals to run with this, to claim that all the old ideas about free trade should be thrown out the window.

In fact, however, few of the international economists responsible for the new trade theory has come out as an advocate of Kuttnerian trade policy. This is not because they are afraid to break the free-trade ranks. It is because the actual prospects for a successful strategic trade policy are not very good.

Once again, this is partly a matter of economics, partly one of politics. On the purely economic side, there just isn't any evidence that an aggressive strategic trade policy can produce large gains. Technological spillovers could be important, but they are difficult to measure. Take the example of HDTV. In the late 1980s there was considerable alarm over the fact that Europe and Japan had taken a commanding lead in the development of HDTV technology. The rhetoric of proponents of a U.S. HDTV program was almost apocalyptic — for example, Senator John Glenn described it as "one of the most, if not the most, crucial technological advancement" in progress. Yet others, such as the Congressional Budget Office, disagreed: "It is hard to believe that HDTV will . . . play a pivotal role in the competitiveness and technological development of the electronics sector." In the end, it all turned out to be a moot point: it soon became apparent that the technologies being developed in Japan and Europe, which transmitted pictures basically the same way as conventional television, were already outmoded in the face of new techniques that sent digital signals and relied on "data compression" to fit the information required for high-definition pictures within the limited bandwidths of existing TV channels. The point, however, is that reaching a practical consensus on which sectors really are strategic is certain to be extremely difficult — even without the interjection of interest-group politics.

As for the possibility of capturing monopoly profits through strategic trade policy, the result of a good deal of technical analysis of the prospects for such policy in particular industries over the past few years is fairly discouraging. The general conclusion of those who have tried to estimate the likely gains from strategic trade policies is that, while you can do better than free trade, the potential net gains are nothing to write home about—they are even smaller than the conventional estimates of the costs of protection. For example, a recent simulation study of the prospects for strategic trade policies in a number of British industries by Anthony Venables of Southampton University found that the potential net gains were generally less than 3 percent of sales.

Meanwhile, there is political reality to consider. Given the uncertainty about what strategic trade policy should be, wouldn't any attempt at doing it turn into thinly disguised interest-group politics? Almost surely it would.

The protectionist prospect

There is a better intellectual case for protection than there used to be, and the case for free trade is often overstated. Nonetheless, there is still a good case for free trade as a general policy—not as an absolute ideal, but as a reasonable rule of thumb. American interests would probably best be served by a world of free trade, with the temptations of strategic trade policy kept out of reach by international treaty. Unfortunately, that's not going to happen, for two reasons.

First, the other major players *are* engaging in strategic trade policy. Quite possibly they are doing themselves more harm than good. But it is extremely difficult to maintain a hands-off position in the United States when other countries do not do the same, especially when America is evidently in relative decline. The extent to which other countries are using strategic policy shouldn't be overstated, but the examples—Japanese protection of supercomputers, European promotion of aircraft—are too conspicuous to dismiss.

Second, the politics of free trade depends on a belief that market access is reciprocal—that open U.S. markets can be traded for open markets elsewhere. For most U.S. trade this has been and remains true. When we negotiated free trade pacts with Canada and Mexico, it meant increased access for both sides; the same would be true if we could negotiate a similar pact with Germany. But free trade becomes very difficult to sustain politically if there is a widespread and growing perception that one of the main players is following different rules.

The problem of relations with Japan—the second largest market economy, one of America's principal trading partners, but an economy into which the United States finds it difficult either to export or invest—is not the most important issue we face, but it is one of the hardest to solve.

11 Japan

An editorial page cartoon in 1987 showed a teacher addressing his history class. "Ironically," says the teacher in the first panel, "during the Second World War we were cooperating with the Soviet Union and fighting with Japan. . . ." In the second panel he continues, ". . . just like today."

It is easy to overstate the seriousness of the tension between the United States and Japan. When Wall Street economist Gary Shilling talks of a shift from Star Wars to Trade Wars, he is making a poor analogy: Trade conflict is a lot less serious than an arms race, let alone a shooting war. Still, the rising hostility of the American public to Japan, and the growing scorn of the Japanese for the United States, will almost surely be the biggest strain on world economic cooperation over the next decade.

Why are the United States and Japan at odds? In many ways the two countries have an economic relationship that provides great mutual benefits. Ask the Washington State loggers who sell their lumber to Japan at twice the price it would fetch on the domestic market, or the U.S. Treasury, which would have to pay far higher rates on the national debt if it were not for the inflow of Japanese capital; and, on the other side, ask Honda, which has half its market in America, or the managers of Japanese pension funds, who get a better return on U.S. bonds than they could get at home.

Yet there is a growing sense among many Americans that Japan is playing the global economic game by different rules from the rest of us. As long as the United States had a comfortable economic and technological superiority over Japan, complaints about Japan were limited to a small group, easily dismissed as representatives of special interests. But with Japan now overtaking the United States in one field after another, the previous murmur of complaint has become a loud clamor.

Meanwhile, the Japanese view it all as simple envy and an attempt to make excuses. They see America as a failing economic power, its competitiveness crippled by social disintegration, racial diversity, poor education, lazy workers, a pervasive emphasis on short-term gains, and a general intellectual and moral flabbiness. To the Japanese, U.S. trade complaints are an attempt to blame our own problems on someone else; their initial dismay has turned into growing anger, and they are increasingly coming to despise us.

Here in America, the lines are already being drawn. A 1989 *Newsweek* story on Japan divided American experts into "apologists" and "bashers"—no middle ground.

But what is the truth? A first step is to ask what is really true about Japan. Only then can we look for answers to the growing tension in U.S.-Japan relations.

The Japanese difference

Does Japan really play by different rules? You might think that this would be a simple question of fact, but it isn't. Instead, it is a source of bitter dispute.

The reason is that there is a wide disparity between the letter of the law and what actually seems to happen in Japan. On paper, Japan's markets are fairly open. Japan is openly and outrageously protectionist when it comes to agricultural goods—

everyone knows about the prices of beef and rice.[9] On manufactured goods, however, Japan's tariff rates are about the same as
those of other industrial countries, and Japan has few of the
"voluntary export restraints" and "orderly marketing agree-
ments" that limit imports of autos, steel, and other goods in both
the United States and Europe. So in international discussions of
trade policy, Japanese officials can describe their nation with a
straight face as a leading practitioner of free trade.

There's only one thing wrong with this picture: If Japan is so
open to the world, how come nobody can sell there?

By now, everyone has heard the anecdotes of businesspeople
trying to sell goods in Japan—of firms that politely refuse to consider your product, even if it is better and cheaper than the local
alternative, of retailers who will not distribute foreign goods.
These anecdotes come mostly from interested parties, and they
might be dismissed as sour grapes if the overall evidence did not
bear them out. For the simple fact is that Japan spends less than
half as much of its income on imports of manufactured goods as
any other advanced nation.

It is important to point out that we are *not* talking about the
fact that Japan runs a large trade surplus in manufactures. Trade
surpluses are ultimately determined by the balance between
domestic saving and investment. Japan runs a large manufactures surplus because it has a very high savings rate, and also
because it *must* run a surplus in manufactures to offset its
imports of raw materials. But it's not the size of the surplus that
makes people accuse Japan of foul play; it's the way that surplus
is achieved, with Japan seemingly a country that exports but
does not import.

---

9. Although it is surprisingly hard to get Japanese to admit even this. I have had the
experience of finding Japanese economists from the private sector refuse to
acknowledge that the rice policy is costly, even in informal conversation. When
pressed hard, they explained that they did not feel it was their place to criticize the
government to a foreigner.

A revealing comparison can be made between Japan and Germany, the third largest market economy. In many ways Japan and West Germany before its reunification with East Germany were similar economies.[10] Both were high-saving countries that exported large amounts of capital to the rest of the world. Both were also crowded countries, with few raw materials, that had to run trade surpluses in manufactures simply to pay for their food and oil. And both ran very large trade surpluses in manufacturing in the 1980s. In fact, as Figure 22 shows, Germany's trade surplus in manufactures was actually larger as a share of its GNP than Japan's.

But there the resemblance ends. Germany is one of the world's greatest markets for imported manufactured goods. The trade surplus came about only because exports were even larger. Germany simply trades more, in both directions. Whatever complaints one may hear about German economic policy, neither the

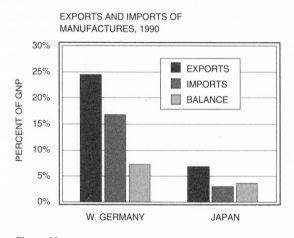

Figure 22
Measured as a share of national income, Germany actually runs substantially larger surpluses in its trade in manufactured goods than does Japan.

10. The German situation has been complicated since 1989 by the reunification of West and East Germany.

Americans nor their fellow Europeans accuse the Germans of having a tacitly closed market.

The Japanese and some of their defenders (like economist Gary Saxonhouse) will reply that the difference is geography: Germany trades so much because it is in the middle of Europe, while Japan is isolated at the edge of Asia. There is some point to this, though with modern transportation and communications, distance is not what it used to be. Even allowing for geography, however, careful analysis of Japan's trade volume suggests that it imports only about half as much as one would expect.[11] The businessman's complaint that the Japanese will not import anything they can make themselves is an exaggeration, yet the overall evidence broadly supports it.

But what limits imports into Japan, when there are only low tariffs and few import quotas? At this point the Japan experts get all fuzzy—which is probably appropriate, because Japan is a fuzzy kind of society, without the hard-edged legalisms that Americans, in particular, expect. Japan hands point to the interlocking structure of ownership within Japan; to the long-term relationships between suppliers, distributors, and banks; to an economy that resembles an elaborate old boys' network more than the free-wheeling markets of America (and which is rife with practices that would be illegal under U.S. antitrust law). For any outsider, this economic structure is hard to break into; for foreigners, it is particularly difficult.

Some foreign experts like to view the Japanese system as not just closed but conspiratorial, tacitly directed by top officials at the Ministry of International Trade and Industry (MITI) and the Ministry of Finance. This is the view advanced by such bashers as Clyde Prestowitz, whose book *Trading Places* portrays a

---

11. The decisive salvo in the academic debate was a 1987 paper on Japanese imports by Robert Lawrence of the Brookings Institution, which showed to the satisfaction of many economists that Japan really does have unexpectedly small imports. It is a measure of the growing polarization in the U.S. debate that *Newsweek* classes Lawrence, who has been an active crusader for free trade, as a "basher."

systematic Japanese pursuit of strategic advantage at America's expense. It is also a view that is increasingly out of date.

There is no question that before the early 1970s the Japanese system was heavily directed from the top, with MITI and the Ministry of Finance influencing the allocation of credit and foreign exchange in an effort to push the economy where they liked. For a long time, however, Japanese firms have had plenty of cash on hand, both foreign and domestic, and a correspondingly greater ability to ignore suggestions from above. Old habits of deference to central authority are still around, but the still popular image of a centralized "Japan Inc." is at least 15 years behind the times. Fashionable current descriptions of Japan, like the recent book of Karel van Wolferen, depict an economy that is characterized neither by free competition nor by central direction, but rather by a web of personal ties and long-term understandings—a conspiracy, if you like, but one without leaders.

Even if there are no central strategists, however, the Japanese economy often appears to be following the very type of strategic

Figure 23
The dollar's fall, which helped the United States to cut its trade deficit with Europe, had little impact on its deficit with Japan.

trade policy that some Americans would like to see adopted here. The ranks of Japanese firms seem to close most strongly against imports of goods that embody new technologies, like supercomputers or what is known in electronics jargon as "amorphous materials." When imports into Japan do increase, as they have since the yen began to rise in 1985, they tend to be either unsophisticated goods or products of the overseas affiliates of Japanese firms, and not the kinds of goods that American firms think they should be able to sell. It is revealing that the falling dollar had a marked effect in shrinking the U.S. trade deficit with Europe but hardly any effect on our deficit with Japan, even though the dollar fell more against the yen than against any other currency.

In sum, then, the widespread perception that Japan plays by different rules is basically right. This is not a moral judgment; it's not a question of what's right or what's fair. It is just a

---

Corporate taxation and foreign direct investment

Somewhat surprisingly, the tax reform of 1986, which, in effect, increased the rate of taxation on corporations, may have been one of the factors that led to a shift of Japanese investment away from passive portfolio investments and toward the direct acquisition of U.S. firms.

In 1981, the United States offered generous depreciation allowances that cut effective corporate tax rates sharply. Somewhat paradoxically, this acted as a disincentive for Japanese firms to own U.S. corporations. When a Japanese firm owns a U.S. corporation, it must eventually pay taxes to the Japanese government on any profits its subsidiary sends home—with a credit for taxes paid to the U.S. government. This meant that Japanese-owned firms, unlike U.S.-owned firms, could not realize the full benefits of the lower tax rate, since the gain from the lower tax rate here was partially offset by the reduced tax credit at home. Thus the low corporate tax rates of 1981–86 had the effect of making corporations more valuable in U.S. than in Japanese hands.

The 1986 tax reform, which raised the effective corporate tax rate, eliminated this bias toward domestic ownership, and may therefore have played a role in the surge of Japanese acquisitions of U.S. firms that followed.

statement of fact. Japan's market is not open to foreigners in the way that U.S. or German markets are open.

The Japanese are coming!

As trade conflict between the United States and Japan grew in the mid-1980s, U.S. officials tried to buy time, hoping that a fall in the dollar eventually would take the pressure off. As it turned out, however, the lower dollar, while quite effective elsewhere, had virtually no effect on U.S.-Japan trade. And partly as a result, a new source of tension has arisen: Japanese direct investment in the United States.

Japan has been investing heavily abroad, largely in the United States, since 1982—a net capital outflow that is the inevitable counterpart of Japan's balance-of-payments surpluses. Until 1986, the Japanese characteristically put their money into "portfolio" investments that yielded income but not control: Treasury bills, corporate paper, and minority stock positions. Then, for reasons that are still controversial, they changed their approach. Even as the overall rate of Japanese investment abroad tapered off, more and more of it took the form of foreign direct investment: investment aimed at establishing operational control. The purchase of Columbia Pictures by Sony made headlines, but it was just one conspicuous example of a broad surge.

The numbers show the surge clearly. In 1985, Japan parked three-quarters of its foreign investment in passive sources of income; by 1989 two-thirds of its investment flows were used to acquire or extend control. The United States, as the world's leading capital importer, has provided the counterpart: Where in the early days of our trade deficit we were able to finance it mostly by selling debt, by the late 1980s we were selling whole firms. Many of these sales were to countries other than Japan—British direct investment is still larger than that of Japan—but Japanese firms in the United States grew rapidly.

Why is this happening now? One reason is the fall in the dollar, which has made the cash resources of Japanese firms look large relative to the prices of U.S. firms. The tax reform act of 1986 may also have inadvertently opened the floodgates. (See box, page 00.) Also, sheer herd instinct may have played a role: Once a few Japanese firms had shown the way, others rushed to follow.

The more important question is whether it is anything to worry about. Twenty years ago, when U.S. multinational corporations were growing in Europe, many Europeans feared that the "American challenge" would overwhelm them. In the end, U.S. investment in Europe did not grow without limit, and U.S. firms in Europe soon came to be regarded as perfectly acceptable corporate citizens. Won't the same turn out to be true of Japanese firms in the United States?

Well, maybe. But here as elsewhere Japan looks different, enough so to cause some worries. If you want to find cause for alarm about the Japanese invasion, there are two facts that can give the complacent pause. First, while Japanese firms invest abroad, Japan itself seems to be a very hard place in which to

COMPOSITION OF JAPANESE INVESTMENT FLOW

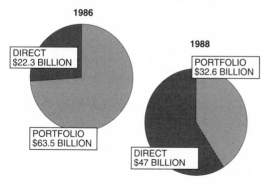

Figure 24
Since 1986 Japan has increasingly used its accumulation of assets abroad not simply to yield returns but also to buy control.

invest—so Japanese firms may have a strategic advantage over
their foreign rivals in the form of a protected home base. Second,
Japanese firms in the United States appear to behave differently
from other firms.

The apparent inability of foreign firms to operate on a large
scale in Japan is an even more striking fact than Japan's resis-
tance to imports. Figure 25 compares the role of foreign-owned
firms in Japan with their role in other advanced countries.
Europeans have long been accustomed to the idea of working
for foreign employers, having a substantial part of the capital
stock foreign-owned, and so on; with growing foreign direct
investment in the United States, America increasingly looks similar. But Japan is barely touched by foreign firms.

Japan's situation with regard to direct investment is like its
situation with regard to imports, only more so. *De jure,* Japan is
wide open; while the government does have some power to
block foreign investments, that power is rarely used. *De facto,*
foreign firms in Japan face endless informal obstacles.

The point is that with Japan now one of the world's great economic powers, the asymmetry of access—Japanese firms can

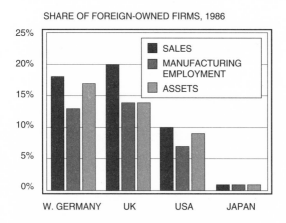

Figure 25
Foreign-owned firms now play an important role in all major industrial countries–
except Japan, where their role remains of minimal importance.

invest abroad, but foreign firms find it difficult to invest in Japan—gives firms of Japanese origin a kind of strategic advantage that is not negligible.

But what difference does it make? Why not accept Japanese firms abroad?

The first wave of Japanese direct investment in the United States saw the creation of manufacturing subsidiaries—first in color televisions, then in autos. To optimists, these investments seemed a clear plus from an American point of view: new plants, new jobs, domestic production in place of imports. Admittedly, there was always a concern that Japanese production would displace domestic autos instead of imports; but on the whole most people looked favorably on these "greenfield" investments.

The wave of investment since 1986 has not, however, followed this earlier model. The Japanese have not for the most part been building new plants. Instead, they have been acquiring existing U.S. enterprises. Bridgestone, a Japanese firm, bought Firestone; Sony bought Columbia Pictures. When a Japanese firm buys an existing American firm, we have to ask whether that firm will be run differently, and if so, whether the U.S. economy will be hurt or helped by the difference.

The optimistic view is that the Japanese will buy firms that they know they can run better than the original management, and so the result will be an increase in efficiency. The Japanese auto companies have shown that they can run plants in the United States at Japan-ese levels of productivity, raising the efficiency of the U.S. labor force both directly and by shaming Detroit into doing better. Surely they will do the same in other industries, and to that extent will help the U.S. economy (although whether Japanese firms can improve the management of the motion picture industry is fairly doubtful).

The pessimistic view is that the Japanese will rearrange their firms to suit Japanese interests, at U.S. expense. Prestowitz and

Robert Reich predict that the Japanese will keep the high-wage activities, the R&D, and much of the sourcing of parts in Japan. The United States, in this view, will be left with "screwdriver" plants where low-wage American workers assemble Japanese products.

Since the great wave of Japanese investment is so recent, it is too early to tell how it will turn out. The behavior of the Japanese firms already here, however, suggests that they are innocent of two of the charges, but guilty of the third. As figure 26 shows, Japanese firms already here actually pay wages as high or higher than both American firms and other foreign firms in the United States; they also do just as much R&D. Unfortunately, the third charge is true: Japanese firms do seem to import a lot more, most of it presumably from Japanese suppliers, than either U.S. firms or other foreign firms. On average, foreign firms in the United States import more than twice as much per worker as American firms; Japanese firms import well over twice as much as the average foreign firm.

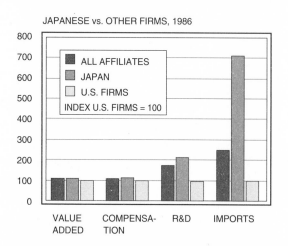

Figure 26
Japanese-owned firms in the United States look similar to U.S.-owned firms and firms owned by other countries in terms of value-added per worker, wages, and spending on R&D. However, they have a much higher tendency to buy inputs from abroad.

It is possible to make excuses for this high propensity to import. In particular, the imports of Japanese subsidiaries may reflect their sheer newness, the lack of time to build up a local supply network. On the other hand, a tendency to buy from their regular suppliers, even when it might be cheaper to source locally, is just what one would expect given the other things we know about Japanese industry. (Some recent comparisons of the behavior of Japanese firms in Australia with those from other countries reveal the same Japanese reluctance to buy either locally or on the world market.)

So here is the case against Japanese multinationals, if you want to make it: They have a strategic advantage against the rest of the world because of their protected home base, and they use this advantage to pursue a buy-Japanese policy even when they acquire production facilities abroad. Perhaps the advantages of attracting Japanese firms outweigh these complaints. But in the highly charged atmosphere of the 1990s it is inevitable that Japanese investment will draw the same kind of lightning as Japanese trade—and perhaps more so.

How much of a problem is it?

During the 1970s it was popular for radicals both in the Third World and in the United States to blame the industrial nations, and America in particular, for the backwardness of the rest of the world. Someone once wrote of these radicals that they seemed to see America as a kind of spacecraft, shooting death rays at the Third World's economy. Few people would now portray the United States that way, but increasingly that is the way Americans seem to view Japan.

How much of a problem does "the Japanese difference" pose for the United States? To defenders of Japan, and to those who believe that a restructured American economy is about to enter a golden age, there is no problem at all. To alarmists like Prestowitz, Japan's challenge is undermining America's economic prospects. The reality is more mundane. The Japanese difference hurts the American economy, but only a little. If our prospects are not too good, the fault lies not in Tokyo but in Washington and New York. The Japan problem is real, but it is not central.

The reason is simple. The main thing that matters for American living standards is still our own productivity. Foreign trade and foreign competition can only make a difference at the margin. If Japan's economy were more open, if Japanese firms abroad were better local citizens, we might be able to trade U.S. goods and services for imports at better terms. Our real income would therefore be higher. But it would be only a marginal improvement. The reasons for our disappointing economic performance lie overwhelmingly in our own shortcomings.

The flip side is also true: Japan's success does not in any important way rest on predatory behavior against the rest of the world. Japan saves six times as high a fraction of its income as the United States and educates its children better than we do. This year Japanese industry will invest more in total than U.S. industry, even though Japan has only half our population. These are sufficient reasons for Japan to grow far faster than the United States, whatever our trading relations. Indeed, it is worth remembering that Japan's economy is not, popular myth to the contrary, primarily an export machine: Japan exports only 14 percent of what it produces, less than any other major industrial country except the United States. It is no wonder that the Japanese are scornful of Americans who want to claim that Japan's success is somehow "stolen" at America's expense.

So it is important to keep a sense of perspective about the Japan problem. Japan is not our nemesis. Japan's success hurts our pride far more than it hurts our standard of living.

Yet there is still a Japan problem. Japan is a great economic power that does not play by the same rules as the other great economic powers. Economically and, above all, politically, that is a fact that cannot be ignored. One way or another, the United States has got to find a way of dealing with Japan.

What to do

There are two extreme views about what to do about Japan. On one side are the old-time free traders, who want us in effect to turn the other cheek. On the other side are the bashers, who want us to confront Japan and demand massive change, or else. So emotional has the dispute between these factions become that it has descended to the level of *ad hominem* charges—free traders accused of getting money from the Japanese, bashers accused of getting money from protectionist special interests. But let's look at the case on the merits.

The free traders—led by economists like Herbert Stein of the American Enterprise Institute and Jagdish Bhagwati of Columbia University—start with the general presumption that free trade is the best economic policy for a country, whatever the rest of the world does. There is an old saw in trade theory: Saying that my country should be protectionist because other countries are is like saying that, because other countries have rocky coasts, I should block up my own harbors. They predict that any kind of confrontation with Japan will end up delivering U.S. trade policy into the hands of our own special interest groups who will wrap their selfish demands in the flag. These free traders also either discount the claims that Japan's *de jure* open markets are not open *de facto*, or adopt the legal view that internal institutional arrangements are not the business of trade law. They then argue that the United States should see to it that our own trade is as free as possible, urge other countries to do the same, and then sit back and enjoy the benefits.

The bashers, of course, view it all very differently. They see large costs to America from the asymmetry with Japan. While their gut feelings may come from conventional mercantilist sentiments, the more sophisticated bashers have learned to employ some of the modern arguments against unilateral free trade that are now current in economic theory. And the bashers therefore call for presentation of an ultimatum to Japan: Change your ways, or else!

For those in neither camp, the whole issue is agonizing. The old-time free trade position seems naive, reflecting neither the realities of Japan nor the political possibilities for America. Yet the basher program seems equally unappealing. Above all, it is virtually certain to fail in its premise: Japan will not suddenly change, and we will therefore be stuck with the "or else."

The point is that if Japan is a conspiracy, it is not a centrally directed one. There is no small group of men in Tokyo who can deliver a liberal Japanese trading regime over the course of a couple of years. Americans often find it hard to believe that Japan is a real country, with real politics, where the average member of parliament is much more concerned with pleasing his constituents (and his campaign contributors) than with keeping America mollified.

So the result of any attempt to force a radical opening of Japan's markets with the threat of U.S. protectionism will be either an embarrassing and politically costly retreat or a situation in which we must carry out our threat. Down that road lies the prospect of a fragmentation of the world into mutually protectionist trading blocs—a costly outcome though not a tragic one.

Is there a middle way? Perhaps not. It seems likely that the bashers will more or less have their way, and that this decade will be one of growing economic nationalism.

My own proposal is that we adopt an explicit, but limited, U.S. industrial policy. That is, the U.S. government should make a decision to frankly subsidize a few sectors, especially in the high-technology area, that may plausibly be described as "strategic," where there is a perceived threat from Japanese competition. It is possible that the costs of such a policy would exceed its economic benefits. But the downside would be limited: Federal expenditures of, say, $10 billion a year to support industrial R&D consortia would produce at least some benefits. So at worst the net cost of the program to the economy would be a few billion dollars a year—or less than one-tenth of 1 percent of GNP.

A limited industrial policy of this sort would also serve two important political purposes: answering those who fear that Japanese strategic trade policy is squeezing the United States out of crucial economic sectors; and providing an incentive for the Japanese to find ways to open up their system—if only to persuade the United States not to subsidize industries that compete with Japanese exports. Moreover, an on-budget program would be less likely to become a special-interest pork barrel than a program of "managed trade," where the costs consist of higher prices that are virtually invisible to consumers.

It is important to emphasize that I am *not* advocating some form of managed trade—nor would managed trade be an acceptable second best alternative to this sort of limited industrial policy. One of the main purposes of this proposal is precisely to provide an alternative to managed trade, with its hidden costs and near-total dominance by interest-group politics.

Viewed from the right perspective, then, a limited U.S. industrial policy could be a relatively cheap way to cope with the stresses produced by relative U.S. decline and the special problem of dealing with Japan. It is unlikely, however, that such a clean solution will be adopted. Instead, the political system is much more likely to adopt some form of "managed trade" via import quotas. Bashers like Kuttner prefer managed trade, perhaps because its costs are less identifiable than straightforward subsidies; politicians prefer it for the same reason. And in the current political environment anything that raises the current budget deficit is avoided, whatever its future costs.

IV   Financial Follies

By the standards of the hysterical late 1970s and early 1980s, the economy since 1985 has been remarkably calm. Inflation has subsided to levels that cause little discomfort; the trade deficit has fallen to a level that can be sustained for a very long time; even the budget deficit, though it surged alarmingly for several years during the recession, now seems once again more or less under control. And the recession, although it cost millions of people (including George Bush) their jobs, was mild compared with the wrenching slump of 1979-82.

Yet for those who make their living from financial markets, the late 1980s and early 1990s were anything but a quiet time. The volume of transactions on world markets has swelled to unprecedented levels. There is now more trading of foreign exchange on a typical day than there was in a month a dozen years ago. The ups and downs of financial markets of the 1980s rival or surpass anything seen before: The 1987 stock market crash was bigger and more global than the Great Crash of 1929; when the European Monetary System broke up in 1992, speculators moved tens of billions of dollars in a matter of days.

Why has the world of finance become so hyperactive? There is no single answer. Yet much of the explanation surely lies in the same persistence of trade deficits and especially inflation that has preoccupied economic policy. Inflation, for instance, has gradually undermined some traditional economic institutions. The rise of inflation essentially bankrupted a large number of savings and loans—and Washington's failure to face up to this fact turned what was initially a relatively modest problem into a fiscal nightmare. Persistent inflation, interacting with the tax system, encouraged corporations to replace equity with debt—a process bound up with the boom in takeovers and buyouts, and with the restructuring of the economy that the trade deficits helped make necessary. And in an attempt to gain credibility in their fight against inflation, European nations tried to commit themselves to fixed exchange rates—an effort that began with surprising success, but ended in political and economic debacle.

To complete our picture of the economy, then, we look at three scenes from the financial world: the savings and loan affair, in which seemingly technical policy issues turned into a financial mess of startling size; the takeover and buyout boom, which more than anything else defined the spirit and style of the 1980s; and the turbulent but (for the United States) surprisingly peripheral events on global financial markets.

12 The Savings and Loan Scandal

The conservative economic program launched by Ronald Reagan in the 1980s had two main elements. One was lower taxes; the other was deregulation—getting the government out of the private sector's way. While most economists were skeptical about the effectiveness of tax cuts for stimulating the economy, deregulation commanded wide support. Even liberal economists were persuaded by the arguments of reformers that everyone could gain from deregulation of airlines, trucking, and banking.

Yet the biggest single economic policy disaster of the 1980s sprang from a misguided attempt at deregulation. Deregulation of the savings and loan industry turned what might have been a $15 billion problem at the beginning of the decade into a burden on the taxpayers at least 10 and perhaps 20 times as great by the decade's end. Of course, the reasons for this debacle went deeper than simple misguided deregulatory zeal. But the rhetoric of economic freedom helped mask what might otherwise have been seen as an obviously irresponsible policy.

Origins of the crisis

Once upon a time, there was a staid, familiar institution called a savings and loan. Savings and loans were created to give ordinary people a safe way to store their money while earning modest interest. To secure the safety of this money, S&L deposits were insured by a federal agency, the Federal Savings and Loan Insurance Corporation, or FSLIC.

From the beginning, it was realized that insuring deposits created a potential source of risk and corruption. A banker whose deposits are publicly insured does not have to prove that his bank is sound. If he offers potential depositors an interest rate that is just slightly above the market rate, they will put their money in his bank, no questions asked—for they know that they cannot lose their money.

But a license to borrow as much as you like, at a fixed interest rate, is a license to gamble. Open a savings and loan; offer an interest rate a little above going rates to attract a lot of deposits; and invest the money you get in the riskiest projects you can find. If the projects work out, great—you've made a lot of money. If not, and the bank does not have enough money to repay its depositors—well, that's FSLIC's problem, not yours. It's heads you win, tails the taxpayers lose. Without the insurance, of course, your depositors would want to check on what kind of investments you were making, and if they thought you were taking too many risks, they would refuse to put money in your bank. With the insurance, they don't care.

This is an obvious problem, and until 1981 it was met with the obvious answer: eligible investments were tightly regulated and individual S&Ls were regularly audited. Lending was largely restricted to homebuyers under rules designed to prevent excessive risk taking. It was an exchange of a privilege (deposit insurance) for a responsibility (low-risk investing). And until the mid-1970s it worked quite well.

What went wrong was a risk that nobody had counted on: inflation. During the 1970s, inflation soared, and market interest rates rose along with it. At first, savings and loans simply lost depositors as the interest rates they paid grew less and less competitive with those offered by banks and money market funds. This problem was solved by allowing S&Ls to pay higher rates, but this only created a new problem. To hold their depositors, S&Ls were obliged to pay interest rates of 8, 9, or 10 percent. Meanwhile, their assets consisted of 30-year home loans made at 4, 5, or 6 percent in the days before inflation began to climb. Instead of lending out money at a higher rate than they paid on deposits, which is what banks are supposed to do, S&Ls found themselves paying more on deposits than they were earning on their assets. By 1980 many S&Ls were clearly in danger of going bankrupt.

Under the rules of the game that were supposed to be in place, this was where FSLIC was expected to do its job. Through nobody's fault, many S&Ls had made investments that in retrospect were a mistake. The solution? Shut them down, pay off their depositors, and let FSLIC cover the difference between what they had and their obligations. Estimates by economists like Robert Litan of the Brookings Institution suggest that about $15 billion in federal money would have allowed the liquidation of those S&Ls that were in real trouble, and thus ended the story.

But that's not what happened.

Double or nothing, 1981–89

The S&L story after 1980 is a simple one. Neither Congress nor the administration wanted to swallow the cost of shutting down bankrupt S&Ls. So they elected to play double or nothing: to offer the entire S&L industry a more favorable deal in return for staying in business, hoping that the problem would go away. Instead, predictably, the problem got worse.

That's not how it was portrayed at the time, of course. The ostensible purpose of the change in the rules announced in 1981 was to allow S&Ls to make more productive use of their money by substantially deregulating the investments they could make—a change justified on the general principle of free markets. But a real move to free markets would have removed the privilege of deposit insurance as the price of deregulation of investment. What the thrifts got, instead, was freedom without responsibility. They now had the right to make risky investments, while continuing to be able to assure depositors that their money was guaranteed by the federal government.

In the short run, this worked. S&Ls received a new injection of capital from high-roller entrepreneurs who were willing to maintain payments to depositors in exchange for the opportunity to gamble with their money. And S&Ls either became risk takers or were bought by people who were. All across the country savings and loans became financiers of speculative developments, projects that could conceivably make a lot of money but were more likely to lose it.

If the economy had boomed through the whole decade, if oil prices had stayed high, if real interest rates had not risen so much, it is just possible that this game of double or nothing might have worked. But, instead, oil prices collapsed, taking the price of Texas real estate with them, and the economy passed through a massive recession. Even after the recovery real interest rates remained much higher than before. By 1989 the S&Ls were in far worse shape than they had been in 1981; closing down the really troubled ones would now cost at least $166 billion. Even allowing for inflation, the real burden to the taxpayers was at least six times as high as it would have been had the S&L problem been dealt with at the beginning of decade.

Apportioning the blame

When the size of the S&L mess became apparent, sensational stories about the abuses of the 1980s hit the press. Tales of bank owners living high at the bank's expense, of corrupt deals, of wild risk taking made exciting reading. Yet it is not clear that the American public has absorbed the real story of what happened.

Reading the press accounts, one might imagine that what happened was some kind of mysterious invasion of immoral men—Jimmy Stewarts run out of their offices by conniving J. R. Ewings. Many of the press stories, aside from moralizing, placed the blame on the regulators for failing to keep an eye on their charges. And surely there was plenty of both corruption and malfeasance. But emphasizing these misses the point, just as focusing on the evil of the Medellín cartel misses the point of the drug problem. The great bulk of the losses came from taking bad risks, not from literal theft. And besides, Americans in general are neither better nor worse people than they used to be. So the real question has to be: What made socially destructive behavior in this industry so much more attractive than it used to be?

We already know the answer. The partial deregulation of the early 1980s made it possible for S&Ls to gamble with their depositors' money, with the federal government absorbing the risks. An S&L was worth more in the hands of a gambler than in the hands of a prudent business manager. So the owners of S&Ls either learned to be high-rollers, or were bought out by individuals who already were. Not surprisingly, the class of people who were temperamentally suited to take advantage of the opportunities offered by privilege without responsibility contained more than its share of rogues and criminals. Yet the epidemic of white-collar crime in the thrift industry was a result of the environment the government created, not an independent event.

Locking the barn door

Regulators, congressional staffers, and economists have always known the answer to the savings and loan problem: Tighten the restrictions on the S&Ls, and require the owners to put in more capital if they want to stay in business. If the capital is not forthcoming, close them down (and pay off the depositors). This was the right answer even in 1980; it is even more obviously the right answer today.

Yet this obvious answer has been avoided by both the administration and Congress for nearly a decade. Even the S&L bailout scheme negotiated in 1989 was only a partial fix: It left the capital requirements on the thrifts too low and failed to allocate enough money to close down all the institutions that need to be shut. This will stretch out the problem for years to come—and quite possibly cost the taxpayers scores of billions of dollars in avoidable future payments. The whole S&L story is one of almost incredibly irresponsible federal policy, repeated year after year, and it still goes on.

Why? The U.S. government fell into two traps; it is hard to say which is the more disreputable.

First, any subsidy program, no matter how costly to the economy, creates a vested interest in its continuance. For most of the past decade there has existed a set of policies that allow shrewd operators to gamble with public funds; these operators are prepared to oppose the loss of their privileges. Given the style of the people who have come to populate the industry, they are also prepared to push their political case with a brashness and disregard for propriety that more established, genteel interest groups avoid. In the long run, the aggressiveness of the S&L industry undercuts its credibility, and threatens too many of its political allies with scandal. But the people we are talking about are not interested in the long run, and in the short run their lavishness can be effective. So the federal government has created a sort of Frankenstein monster of political economy, which may still devour many billions of dollars before it is slain.

Second, shutting the S&Ls down costs money. Worse yet, even as the foolishness of going on with double or nothing has grown, the cost of stopping the game has risen—and the restraints of federal budget cutting have grown. In the 1989 thrift plan the problem was finessed by putting the expenditures off-budget, but the trickery is straining the whole process.

What makes this sad is that paying off the depositors now is not really a cost to the taxpayers, because that cost has already been incurred. The real decision to spend taxpayer money was made long ago, when the federal government chose to encourage risk taking by institutions whose downside was publicly insured. The real cost of that decision to the economy took place when the dubious investments made by these institutions went bad; paying the depositors off now is simply giving them money they already think they have. Paying the cost of closing the S&Ls now only recognizes these costs.

There is no case for putting off the inevitable—not even concern about national saving. Even if the federal government must borrow the money with which to pay off the S&L depositors, it will not by any calculation have a negative effect on national saving. The depositors will not feel any richer—they thought they had that money anyway—so they will not increase their consumption. Meanwhile, by stopping the game, the federal government will cut its future losses. This is a clear case where the efforts of the government to avoid increasing the *measured* deficit actually aggravate the problems that deficit reduction is supposed to cure.

Is there more to come?

The S & L story is not completely over, but the main costs of cleanup have probably already been paid. The interesting and worrying question is whether the S & L story is part of a broader pattern of hidden federal liabilities.

The answer is surely yes. The S & L story is only the most extreme case of a broader phenomenon.

Start with the rest of the banking system, and in particular the commercial banks—firms like Citibank or Chase Manhattan that specialize in lending to businesses. These banks were subject to many of the same forces that led to the S & L debacle. Their profitability was eroded during the 1970s by inflation and deregulation; since they were no longer highly profitable, they were tempted to make risky loans; and the federal government encouraged them to do so by relaxing restrictions on their investment. The result was a lot of questionable lending, especially of two kinds: financing for financial schemes like leveraged buyouts, and financing for speculative real estate deals. By 1991 a number of reasonable people were warning that there might have to be a commercial bank rescue similar to the S & L bailout, with a price tag of $50-100 billion.

At the time of writing this crisis had been postponed if not necessarily avoided—but only through sheer luck. The attempts of the Federal Reserve to pull the U.S. economy out of a stubborn recession had led to very low short-term interest rates. Since these rates determine the interest rates that banks have to pay on deposits, the paradoxical result was a surge in bank profitability. Still, this windfall gain doesn't contradict the conclusion that misregulation was doing some peculiar things to bank lending during the 1980s.

There are also a number of other, fairly obscure government policies that produce hidden future liabilities. For example, there is an institution called the Pension Benefit Guarantee Corporation, which guarantees corporate pension plans in much the same way that FSLIC guaranteed thrift deposits. It turns out that there are incentives for companies to set aside insufficient money for their pension plans, then dump the problem in PBGC's lap; the federal Office of Management and Budget has estimated that there may be a hidden federal liability of $30-40 billion.

This sounds like a lot of money. Compared with the $3 trillion of additional federal debt run up during the 1980s, however, it is not that impressive. As Everett Dirksen once said about the federal budget, a billion here, a billion there, and soon you're talking about real money. The same surely applies here. If we are trying to assess the impact on our $6 trillion economy, however, it seems unlikely that any of the remaining hidden financial liabilities of the U.S. government will prove a devastating burden.

13   Corporate Finance

The August 1989 issue of *Fortune*, to the titillation of its readers, featured a story on the "CEO's second wife." On the cover was Carolyne Roehm, a glamorous former model and fashion designer. The article was revealing in many ways about the state of American society at the end of the 1980s, but one of the more unintentional lessons came in the choice of cover girl. For Roehm's husband is not a captain of industry in the traditional sense. He is Henry Kravis, driving force behind the investment firm of Kohlberg Kravis Roberts—a specialist in takeovers and leveraged buyouts. That is, Kravis has made his huge personal fortune not by building a productive enterprise in the usual sense, but by mediating in the rearrangement of existing firms' ownership.

This choice is no accident. The 1980s were an era in which fabulous fortunes were made in corporate finance. The heroes of the age were the entrepreneurs, people like Apple's Steve Jobs or Lotus's Mitch Kapor. But the really big money went to the deal makers. If the late nineteenth century was the era of the robber barons, the 1980s were to an even greater extent that of the Financial Wizards. Indeed, the achievements of the sudden rich of the 1980s in many ways eclipsed those of the robber barons. The great nineteenth-century fortunes grew slowly, along with the enterprises they were tied to: mile by mile of railroad, steel mill by steel mill, refinery by refinery. The great fortunes of the 1980s came swiftly, sometimes in a matter of weeks, and often while their owners were still young enough to enjoy them to the fullest (hence the *Fortune* article).

The emergence of sudden wealth in the financial markets is one of the great spectacles of the age. We cannot understand our economy without understanding what it means. Specifically, we need to answer three questions. First, where did the wealth come from? Second, why did a few individuals profit so massively? Third, why did it all happen in the 1980s?

Where did the wealth come from?

The financial operations that created so much wealth for a few Americans require much more than a random reshuffling of paper. Indeed, they involved two systematic changes in the structure of American industry. On one side, there was a substantial shift in *control,* away from either the original owners or the original management. On the other, there was a massive shift in *financing,* away from equity and toward debt.

What financial operators do is to facilitate the purchase of part or all of an existing company either by another company (a takeover) or by a group of investors that often includes the original management (a leveraged buyout, or LBO).[12] In either case the result is a shift of control. In a takeover the original management is displaced by the management of the acquiring firm. In an LBO the hired management stays, but the original board of directors is cut out.

Both takeovers and LBOs typically involve the creation of considerable amounts of corporate debt. The investors in an

12. In practice, many financial deals involve both LBO and takeover elements. For example, the group that buys a firm in an LBO may immediately sell off parts of the firm to other firms in order to pay off part of the debt they have just taken on.

LBO do not usually have enough money to pay for the company out of their own pockets; they must borrow the money. The acquiring corporations in takeover battles also usually come up with the cash by borrowing. So both takeovers and LBOs lead to sharp increases in corporate debt. On the other side, the total quantity of corporate stock outstanding falls, as the stock is bought up by the acquiring firm or group of investors. The 1980s were marked by a combination of large new issues of corporate debt together with a large *negative* net rate of issue of equity.

Both operations are also typically very expensive. Stock bought in either a takeover or an LBO typically sells for a premium of more than 50 percent over its previous market price. To this must be added substantial fees to the investment firms that arrange the deal. So a number of people make a lot of money. The original stockholders are paid substantially more than their stock was initially selling for. And the investment houses get enough to pay for a lot of expensive houses, parties, and, apparently, wives. The question is: Where does all this money come from?

Like so many issues in the past decade, this is a matter of bitter dispute among the experts. Within a five-minute walk from Cambridge's Harvard Square one can find the chief exponents of two radically opposed views.

The optimistic view is that of the Harvard Business School's Michael Jensen. According to Jensen, the rise in stock prices associated with the shift in control represents a gain in efficiency. That is, the new owners of a firm will simply manage the firm better than the people they replace. The market understands this, so when it sees that a takeover or LBO is imminent, it raises its estimation of what the stock is worth.

A much more pessimistic view has been expounded by Jensen's Harvard colleague Lawrence Summers—chief economic adviser to the ill-fated Dukakis presidential campaign and now

a top official at the treasury department. Summers argues that
the gains come not from raising efficiency but by taking money
away from others. Summers and Andrei Shleifer of the
University of Chicago claim that the bulk of the rise in stock
prices in takeovers and LBOs comes from "breach of contract"—
from breaking promises made by the original owners or management in return for past favors. This is the Gordon Gekko
image from the movie *Wall Street*: Financial operators get rich by
slashing wages, by firing workers who had been promised job
security, and by taking on a debt burden that exposes existing
holders of corporate debt to an unanticipated risk of bankruptcy.

Which of these views makes the most sense? Let's look at
them in a bit more detail.

Efficiency gains

Michael Jensen has taken on the role of the chief academic
defender of takeovers and LBOs. In his view, the gain to stockholders from corporate reshufflings is a gain to the economy;

Figure 27
During the 1980s corporations issued large amounts of debt, while repurchases of
stock greatly exceeded new issues.

indeed, he likes to count up the increases in stock prices resulting from takeovers and LBOs and use the number as a measure of the contribution of investment houses to America's economic growth.

Where does Jensen think the gains come from? It's not that the acquiring managers are necessarily smarter than the people they replace. The potential for gain comes from the fact that managers traditionally have had too much independence. According to Jensen, in many corporations management has ceased to serve the interests of the shareholders. Top management hoards retained earnings to invest in projects that increase its power and perks instead of returning them to the stockholders; they invest in low-return but prestige-building ventures; they accept wasteful labor practices and poor management at lower levels rather than face unpleasant confrontations. How can they get away with this? Because stockholders are too scattered and diverse a group to be fully informed about management's actions, or to act effectively if they are informed. Jensen argues that since the typical premium in a financial restructuring is 50 percent, the typical management was wasting about 30 percent of the stockholders' rightful returns.

Into this sloppy management setting come the new financial artists. They put control of the corporation into aggressive new hands—or, by making the managers the new owners, put new fire in their bellies. They also place the corporation under a debt burden that requires the managers to maximize profits simply to meet interest payments. The result? A new dedication to efficiency that makes millions for its engineers, but justifiably so, because it revitalizes the firm.

What's wrong with this vision? While many people feel instinctively comfortable with the idea that the typical corporate management is lazy, self-aggrandizing, and generally unlikable, it is a little hard to believe that the observed stock premiums result solely from efficiency gains due to paper restructurings.

And surely the crucial question must be why, if corporate restructuring is so beneficial, the great wave of restructuring since 1980 didn't have a more noticeable effect on America's economic growth. Hundreds of billions of dollars were added to stock prices through such deals. Yet productivity growth was hardly faster than in the 1970s, and America's economic and technological standing in the world continued its inexorable decline. If we're so rich, why aren't we smarter?

Jensen himself seems insensitive to some of the ironies involved in the divergence between stock prices and other measures of economic performance. In a paper presented to the 1988 "Predator's Ball" sponsored by Drexel Burnham Lambert (former home of junk bond king and convicted insider trader Michael Milken), he provided a glowing portrait of the new, efficient corporate structures made possible by takeovers and LBOs. He then contrasted this happy modern situation with the bad old days when independent management, unaccountable to stockholders, felt free to squander corporate cash flow—a situation that, according to Jensen, "reached its peak in the mid to late 1960s." It did not seem to bother him that his bad times in the mid to late 1960s were an era of 3 percent annual productivity growth, rapidly rising living standards, and U.S. technological preeminence, while his modern era of efficiency was a time of 1 percent productivity growth, stagnant living standards, and relative decline.

No doubt Jensen is right that a takeover or LBO often produces a gain in economic efficiency. Both popular perception and the views of other experts suggest, however, that much if not most of the gains occur not from increasing wealth but from redistributing it.

Breach of contract

Lawrence Summers and Andrei Shleifer have taken on the role
of "anti-Jensens," producing arguments against the corporate
restructurings of the 1980s. Their case fits popular prejudice better than Jensen's. But let's see how it works.

Summers and Shleifer start with a scenario. Imagine a company that for some reason has long had a policy of paying its
workers more than they could earn elsewhere. Suppose for the
moment that this high-wage policy represents nothing more
than weak management, which buys labor peace at stockholder
expense. Following a corporate restructuring, a new lean, mean
management changes this policy: It demands and gets wage cuts
that raise profits and hence the value of the firm to stockholders.

What Summers and Shleifer point out is that in this case the
rise in the stock price does *not* measure a gain to the U.S. economy as a whole. It simply reflects a redistribution of the existing
pie, away from workers and to the stockholders. You may think
this is a good thing or a bad thing, but either way it is wrong to
follow Jensen's procedure and equate rises in stock prices with
gains to the economy.

Summers and Shleifer claim that most of the added value
from corporate restructuring results from a redistribution of
income rather than an increase in efficiency. Wages are the most
obvious target: In many firms workers are paid more than the
minimum that would keep them from quitting, and the popular
picture surely suggests that wage cuts are a common follow-up
to LBOs and takeovers. Another target is the company's bondholders: By reducing its equity and taking on more debt, a
restructured company can increase the upside potential for profits, while passing some of the downside risk to people who lent
the company money in the past never imagining that the firm
would put itself so deeply into debt. In 1988, when RJR Nabisco

became the target of a leveraged buyout attempt (engineered by Kohlberg Kravis Roberts), the price of its outstanding bonds fell 16 percent.

At the very least, the Summers-Shleifer argument suggests that people like Jensen greatly overstate the gains from corporate restructuring, and that they are very wrong in arguing that almost everyone gains. But Summers and Shleifer go further, and suggest that the long-run effect may well be to make nearly everyone worse off.

Their argument is that most of the benefits taken away from workers and bondholders were not simple giveaways. Instead, they were part of long-term implicit understandings. Firms that pay above-market wages and protect job security do not necessarily do so because their managements are softhearted. They might also do it in exchange for long-term commitment and high morale on the part of their work force. Firms that keep their debt low are protecting their reputation so that they can continue to borrow at favorable rates. In effect, Summers and Shleifer argue, what happens following a corporate restructuring is the breaking of a set of unwritten contracts between a firm and its "stakeholders"—all of those other than its stockholders who have made a long-term commitment to the firm. Such unwritten contracts have no legal force; but then most business dealings are based on trust and on a concern for reputation, rather than on the letter of the law.

According to the breach-of-contract view, the corporate restructurings of the 1980s have produced a new disregard for the maintenance of long-term relationships. This leads to large immediate benefits for stockholders, as income is redistributed in their favor. But in the long run, it will mean that corporations find it harder to build up invisible assets like worker morale. The result will be slower economic growth and a lower standard of living for most Americans.

How does this thesis stand up against the facts? The claim that most of the gains of restructuring come from redistribution is more in harmony with what we know about the American economy in the 1980s than the Jensen view. If Jensen were right, we should have seen a decade of great economic strides in productivity. We didn't. On the other hand, the Summers-Shleifer view would lead us to expect growing income inequality, with declining real wages for previously well-paid blue-collar workers in particular, as the counterpart of higher stock prices. And we have indeed seen all these things.

But their argument that the wage cuts sometimes associated with takeovers represent the breaking of an efficient long-term arrangement is more doubtful. They may be idealizing the past as much as Jensen idealizes the future. At a guess, when the target of a takeover paid premium wages, this was less because it represented an efficient long-term bargain than because sloppy management preferred not to bargain hard with workers.

A compromise view

There is certainly some truth to both the Jensen and Summers-Shleifer views of corporate restructuring. A compromise view might argue that the changing structure of the U.S. economy in the 1980s offered opportunities to raise the value of companies both by raising efficiency and by squeezing wages. Let's consider a story that may be helpful as a way of thinking about what happened.

According to this story, the corporate restructurings of the 1980s were largely motivated by the needs of economic restructuring—specifically, the need to dismantle "smokestack America."

In the 1960s and even during the 1970s, America's economic landscape was still dominated by the great corporations of the industrial heartland, and by the powerful unions that organized their workers. These blue-collar workers commanded wages well above what comparable workers earned elsewhere; but the firms they worked for, with long traditions of avoiding price competition, could easily pass these wage costs on to consumers.

Then came the trade deficit and the intensification of international competition. In the face of this competition it became necessary both to "downsize" smokestack America, withdrawing capital from traditional industrial sectors, and to cut the wages of industrial workers. These were tasks for which the existing management structure was ill suited. The managers of firms in the shrinking traditional industries were unwilling to return their cash flow to stockholders, even if there were higher-return investments available in other industries. Yet they lacked the knowledge to diversify profitably into new areas. They were also unwilling to confront their unions and seek givebacks and wage cuts.

Debt-financed takeovers and leveraged buyouts changed all that. Stockholders were bought out at a premium, and a large debt was incurred to finance the buyout. This debt both enabled and forced a change in management behavior. The burden of debt left managers little surplus cash flow to invest in the wrong place, and enforced a new toughness in labor negotiations. The restructured corporations had to be lean and mean to satisfy their creditors; and their new leanness and meanness retroactively justified the premium prices paid in the takeover.

This story contains elements of both Jensen and Summers. It agrees with Jensen that the value of corporate restructurings comes from the way they change management incentives, and that some of these gains represent a real gain to the economy, as capital is reallocated away from low-return sectors. But it also agrees with Summers that many of the financial gains come not from increased efficiency but from cutting the incomes of previously well-paid workers. Moreover, it establishes a link between the financial fever of the 1980s and the rapid growth of inequality.

Why do some people make so much money?

Whichever Harvard professor is right about the ultimate reasons, the 1980s witnessed a record number of occasions in which a firm or a group of investors came to believe that a corporation was worth substantially more in their hands than in the hands of current management. So it is not surprising that there have been a large number of transactions in which corporations have changed hands.

What is a little more surprising is the exotic new world of financial practice that rapidly emerged around the business of corporate restructuring. This new world included previously unheard-of activities for firms, ranging from "greenmail" to "poison pills," from searches for "white knights" to "Pac-Man defenses." It has also created new professions, like risk arbitrage, which seemed mysteriously lucrative, and turned previously obscure sins, like insider trading, into major sources of concern.

What's all this about? There is neither space nor need to describe all the details here—especially because this is a field in which some of the cleverest people in the country are engaged in developing new variations every day. But a few basic principles may help make sense of the wild new world of corporate finance.

The starting point is a seemingly simple insight on the economics of takeovers by economists Sanford Grossman of the Wharton School and MIT's Oliver Hart. Suppose, said Grossman and Hart in a now famous 1978 paper, that one firm has come to believe that by taking over another it can greatly enhance the target's value—say, that the acquired firm would be worth 50 percent more than the current value of its stock. Suppose also that it offers to buy the target from its stockholders. What price will those stockholders demand? More to the point, how much of the benefit of the takeover will accrue to the bought-out stockholders rather than to the acquiring firm?

The answer, according to Grossman and Hart, is that the stockholders will reap *all* of the benefits, that nothing will be left for the acquirer. As soon as stockholders know that the stock is worth 50 percent above its previous price to the acquirer, they will refuse to sell unless they get that price. So the market price will rise on the news of an impending takeover to a point that makes the takeover only barely worth carrying through.

But the cost of a takeover extends beyond the price of the stock. To prepare for a takeover requires research, time spent lining up financing, and much else. Unfortunately, these costs are already sunk by the time the bid is actually made, and, according to the Grossman-Hart analysis, the stockholders will not leave any margin in the price to help defray them. So according to their model, a takeover bid should always lose money, even if it really can raise the profitability of the target firm.

The Grossman-Hart analysis was intended, among other things, to explain why takeovers used to be relatively rare. In the 1980s, however, takeovers became common. Why? At least part of the answer is that a shrewd acquirer can pick up a substantial part of the target company's stock *before* his intention to attempt a takeover becomes known. This initial stock purchase takes place at a lower price than the subsequent takeover bid, and so dilutes the transfer to the original stockholders. Of course, such a successful initial purchase must be surreptitious. If it becomes known that a potential acquirer is trying to buy a company's stock, the price will rise in anticipation.

Once one understands this need to buy as much of a target firm as possible on the sly, much of the wild world of corporate finance in the 1980s becomes comprehensible. First, the style of today's finance—half military exercise, half little boy's game—can be seen as a logical outgrowth of the dynamics of takeover, in which speed and surprise are essential, and in which getting information and deceiving rivals become the primary routes to success. Second, the new style of finance creates new professions. It has always been true that one could make a lot of money by figuring out what would happen to a company's stock in the near future. That used to require an assessment of the company's prospects. Today, however, the biggest cause of large changes in stock prices is the action of other companies. If you can figure out which companies will be targets of takeover or LBO attempts in the near future, you can achieve quick wealth. And so we have the emergence of risk arbitrage: the practice of buying up the stock of likely targets for restructuring.

How do risk arbitrageurs do their job? In principle, they can rely on careful assessment of the likely strategies of corporations, on movements in stock prices that suggest a takeover bid is in the works, on legally obtained intelligence about the movements and actions of key players. As anyone can see, however, there is another obvious and more certain way to know who is contemplating buying what: Pay someone who knows to tell you. Hence we have the rise of insider trading, the eventual fall of Ivan Boesky and Michael Milken.

We know, then, how some people got rich: The new world of corporate finance both offered new levels of reward to investors who can outguess other investors and created the potential for a new kind of genteel crime. But the inevitably associated activities of risk arbitrage and insider trading need a few further comments.

First, risk arbitrage, even if done honestly, is one of the least productive activities ever devised. It is a sad commentary that some of the smartest, most energetic people in America make very comfortable livings trying to guess what some other smart people will be doing a few hours later. Matters are all the sadder, of course, if these best and brightest employ illegal methods to gain that extra edge.

On the other hand, it may be said that neither risk arbitrage nor even insider trading is inherently damaging to the economy. What does a risk arbitrageur do? He buys stock in the likely target of a takeover or LBO, and therefore makes the takeover more expensive. He is naturally more effective at this if he has inside information. The net effect is to discourage corporate restructurings. If corporate restructurings were always or even usually a good thing, this would be a cause for dismay. But as we have seen, there is a fairly good case against at least some restructurings. So a bit of sand in the wheels is not a great tragedy. It will be a while before Lawrence Summers starts singing the praises of Ivan Boesky, but in a perverse way they are allies.

The potential for abuse of trust built into the current world of corporate finance also helps explain why it pays so well—why freshly minted MBAs earn six-digit salaries, and why the princes of finance are paid sums almost beyond imagining. These are undoubtedly remarkable people, with steel nerves and quick judgment, operating in a business where tiny edges bring huge returns. But they are exposed to severe temptation. Bank managers are well paid, not only for their skills, but also because it is not always a good idea to entrust heavy responsibility to people paid a niggardly salary. Similarly, investment bankers are more reliable if they earn enough, and value their good name enough, to look temptation in the face and pass it by.

Why the 1980s?

Perhaps the most perplexing question about the spectacular restructuring of corporate America in the 1980s is: Why then?

Whether the money came from efficiency gains (just wait and see), stealing the bread of honest workers and bondholders, or suckering gullible dentists who buy junk bonds, why this decade and not before?

Here are a few hypotheses:

First is the argument that Michael Milken produced the times, and not the other way around. Arguably (as Jensen, among others, does argue), the new corporate finance involves important innovations that make it possible for firms to carry more debt than before. (Notice, by the way, that even if this is true, it doesn't mean that buyouts are a good thing; these innovations could be financing breach of contract instead of increased efficiency.)

A second hypothesis is that changes in the political climate cleared the way for the new age. Many of the mergers of the past decade would have faced severe antitrust challenges in the 1970s; others would have brought once powerful unions into action, with tacit support from the federal government. It is certainly a remarkable coincidence that so much new wealth emerged just as the body politic decided that it was OK to get rich. Maybe it wasn't a coincidence.

And there is one more possible explanation. To the extent that the whole enterprise depended on downplaying the risk of junk bond finance, maybe the key was simply that enough time had passed since the last great financial crisis. Harvard's Benjamin Friedman has pointed out that while the risk of financial crisis is roughly constant over time, such crises occur so rarely that an estimate of their probability based only on recent experience will fluctuate between excessive pessimism (in the immediate aftermath of crisis) and totally unwarranted optimism (after a stretch of good luck). So maybe it was just the passage of time that laid the groundwork for the 1980s. Once the great buying spree had started, it became harder and harder for the pessimists to cling to their convictions—and off we went.

And down we came. By the early 1990s, it looked as if the great financial restucturing of the 1980s was indeed powered to a large extent by excessive investor optimism. Many of the companies that took on large quantities of debt in the 1980s found themselves in financial trouble in the 1990s. The result was a virtual collapse of the junk bond market, as investors became disillusioned with the financial instruments Milken had made so popular. One useful measure of that disillusionment was the precipitous drop in the prices of junk bonds on the secondary market (the market in which the debt of companies is traded among third parties): by the end of 1990, the bonds issued during the Milken era were selling on average at only about half their face value. Taking into account these capital losses, it appeared that Milken had actually lost money for his investors.

It's possible that the disillusionment of investors with junk-bond finance in the early 1990s was as much an overreaction as their infatuation with it in the 1980s. Still, the whole story was a sobering lesson in how difficult it is to tell financial genius from sheer hucksterism.

14   **Global Finance**

One of the surprising things about the big financial events in the United States during the 1980s—the savings and loan debacle, the rise and fall of the junk bond market, and such less heralded events as the emergence of huge markets in strange new assets like mortgage-backed securities—was how relentlessly domestic they were. A savings and loan association is a quintessentially American institution, and the scandal was largely played out in the small cities and towns of the American heartland. The wave of leveraged buyouts was largely confined to the United States. Foreign firms increased their stake in the U.S. economy, but they did so largely through friendly acquisitions, not the hostile takeovers favored by our own corporate raiders; and these raiders rarely made forays overseas. The financial excitement of the 1980s was a homegrown affair.

Why was this surprising? Because the word "global" has become a favorite buzzword for commentators on economic affairs. Indeed, it has become almost pro forma for businesspeople to talk in hushed tones about the extraordinary international mobility of capital, which supposedly integrates the world into a seamless whole. Walter Wriston, the former chairman of Citibank, expressed this new conventional wisdom in a 1992 book entitled *The Twilight of Sovereignty: How Information*

Technology is Changing the World, in which he argued that computers and telecommunications, by linking national markets, were making national policymakers increasingly ineffectual.

Much of this is hype. International financial events have been surprisingly peripheral to U.S. economic affairs since 1980. It is hard to think of any shock originating outside the United States since the 1979 surge in oil prices that has had a really major impact on the U.S. economy, and even that had little to do with financial markets. Yet while global financial markets have not had a major impact on actual events, they have fascinated many influential people—and that is in itself a reason to review some of the main features of these markets.

How global is the global market?

On any given day, huge sums of money are moved around the world. Surveys show that during 1989 world foreign exchange transactions, in which individuals and firms convert their funds from one currency into another, exceeded $500 billion every *day*. The vast bulk of these transactions involved purchases of assets rather than goods and services; that is, there were massive international movements of capital.

Nonetheless, in spite of this frenetic pace of business, it would be premature to conclude that national boundaries have become irrelevant. Indeed, in some ways the links between national capital markets are surprisingly weak.

For one thing, while there is a lot of trading, relatively few investors seem willing to make long-term commitments to foreign markets. There is remarkably little international diversification of portfolios—that is, Americans are rarely stockholders of foreign companies, and conversely. Estimates suggest that more than 90 percent of the value of stocks owned by American residents is still in American companies; the same is true of Japanese and European investors.[13]

Perhaps because there is so little international "cross-holding" of stocks, world stock markets do not necessarily move together. This was illustrated spectacularly from 1990 to 1992, when the Japanese stock market—which at its peak was worth more than the U.S. market—began a prolonged slide. Over the course of two years, the Nikkei index fell more than 60 percent. In a closely integrated capital market, one might have thought that such a huge decline in what was at the beginning the world's biggest market would drag down other markets as well. Yet in fact stock prices in the United States and Europe actually rose over the same period.

Finally, there is surprisingly limited long-term capital movement, even when compared with past experience. Japan saved 18 percent of its income in the 1980s, twice the average of other advanced nations. One might have expected the Japanese to invest a large share of those savings abroad. In fact, the average capital outflow was only 2 percent of national income, about 11 percent of total savings. By contrast, the United Kingdom invested 40 percent of its savings abroad over the 40-year period ending in 1913. By this measure, at least, we seem to have a less effective global capital market in the age of computers than we did in the age of steam.

Although the global capital market is less global than we sometimes tend to imagine, it is not totally unimportant. So let's turn to several cases in which international financial events were thought to be crucial by U.S. policymakers.

---

13. Compare this with the situation within the United States: California residents show virtually no preference for owning the stocks of California-based as opposed to, say, New York-based companies.

Third World debt

During the 1970s, private bankers in the United States and else-where decided that lending to Third World countries was a good idea. Loans to governments, or loans guaranteed by govern-ments, looked safe enough to the bankers to make the higher yields on Third World lending attractive—as Citibank's Walter Wriston asserted, in remarks he was later to regret, "Sovereign nations don't go bankrupt."

As long as the flow of money continued, everything looked fine: The debtor countries could pay interest and principal easily out of the new loans. In 1981 and 1982, however, for a variety of reasons, confidence evaporated, and the flow of money dried up with it—and it turned out that the countries could not generate enough cash to service their debt. The result was a rolling crisis that continued through the rest of the decade.

Third World debt figures prominently in many pictures of the world economy in the 1980s. In human terms this is clearly appropriate. Most of Latin America and most of Sub-Saharan Africa, as well as a few other nations like the Philippines, have been hard hit by the debt crisis. Economic growth in the highly indebted countries (HICs) has been far slower since 1981 than before. Unemployment and inflation have soared, living stan-dards of already very poor families have deteriorated. For some of those at the bottom in Latin America (and even more so in Africa), the debt crisis was lethal.

As a concern of U.S. *economic* policy, however, the debt crisis is not a major issue. The unfortunate fact about poor countries is that they don't have much money—and so, in purely economic terms, they do not carry much weight. The combined gross national products of all troubled debtors are less than 4 percent of the world's GNP. The total value of all loans to troubled debtors is less than 1 percent of the wealth of the creditor nations; the debt service on those loans less than one-quarter of 1 percent of the national incomes of the creditors. Terrible as it is to say, the United States does not have a strong economic interest in what happens to Third World debtors.

Nonetheless, for much of the 1980s the problems of Third World debtor countries were a subject of high-level policy concern, for two main reasons.

First, in the early years of the debt crisis there was a fear that defaults by debtor countries could help trigger a banking crisis. Although the sums of money involved were not large compared with the world economy as a whole, claims on troubled debtors were concentrated in the hands of the largest banks; since the onset of the debt crisis coincided with a severe recession in the United States and Europe, policymakers worried that losses in the Third World could tip crucial "money center" banks over the edge. This danger receded as the Western economies recovered; by the late 1980s, bank regulators were much more worried about bad loans to real estate developers than they were about outstanding claims on Brazil or Mexico.

Second, the creditor nations felt that they had an interest in preserving the political stability of debtors, and they feared that a confrontation between debtors and bankers could lead to radicalization. In 1982 the picture of an anti-American movement rising to power in Mexico by denouncing foreign banks and demanding debt repudiation did not seem farfetched. Indeed, it could still happen — not this year or next, but it would be foolish to imagine that resentment of rich nations has vanished from the world.

So officials at the Federal Reserve, the U.S. Treasury, and the International Monetary Fund believed that they had to take a hand in the debt problem. But what was the right policy?

Financing vs. forgiving

Suppose that someone who owes you money approaches you and tells you that he cannot pay in full. After checking out the story, you find that he is telling the truth, and that no purpose would be served by trying to force him to come up with the money. What do you do? You have two basic choices. You can give him time by postponing the payment, in effect lending him the money he cannot pay, and hope that he will be able to pay later. Or you can tell him to pay what he can, and consider the account settled (except that you probably will not lend him money again for a long time). The same basic options confront the creditors of the Third World: They can either *finance* the debt—that is, postpone the countries' obligations and hope that things will look better later on—or they can *forgive* it, reduce the debtors' obligations to a level that they may be able to pay.

From 1982 until 1989, official policy toward Third World debt was based on the premise that financing was enough, that if debtor nations were given time, they would eventually be able to meet their obligations. Then, in March 1989, Treasury Secretary Nicholas Brady declared that the United States was now advocating a strategy of debt reduction.

During the years of the financing strategy, the obligations of countries were postponed in three ways. Repayment of principal was rescheduled; official agencies such as the IMF and the World Bank made new loans to the countries that could be used to pay part of the interest coming due; and the banks that had lent money to the countries in the first place were rounded up for so-called "concerted" lending, which amounted to indirect relending of part of the remaining interest. In effect, repayment of debt was very nearly halted, and limited new lending was arranged from both private and public sources.

This strategy could be, and was, described as a plan to put highly indebted countries still deeper into debt. In the early years of the debt problem, however, this did not seem like a bad idea. Given the rates of growth achieved by debtor nations in the past, and the economic reforms insisted on by the creditors as part of the package, it seemed likely that most of the major debtors could grow their way out of their debt problem. In other words, even though the debt might grow, the incomes of the debtors would grow faster—and thus the creditworthiness of the debtors would improve, not worsen, over time.

By 1989, however, nearly everyone agreed that this strategy had failed. The main problem was that growth in the most heavily indebted countries had simply failed to live up to expectations. The major debtor nations had managed growth rates of 5 percent or more in the years before the crisis. After 1982 they hardly grew at all, which meant that their per capita income fell steadily as their populations increased. It remains uncertain how much of the slowdown was due to the debt crisis itself, but the result was clear: political demands for debt reduction grew within the debtor countries, while the lack of growth discouraged potential investors. The prospect of regaining access to world financial markets seemed more remote than ever: in early 1989 the secondary market price of Third World debt—the price at which creditors sell claims to each other—averaged only 30 percent of face value.

As a result, in 1989 Nicholas Brady, the Secretary of the Treasury, announced U.S. support for a strategy of reducing Third World debt. Within six months Mexico had negotiated a "Brady deal" to reduce its debt; over the next three years most other major debtors followed suit.

And then something strange happened.

The "emerging markets" phenomenon

The debt reductions involved in the Brady deals were not very large. For example, Mexico managed to reduce its debt by only about 10 percent—hardly enough, one might think, to make a big difference to its economic situation. And yet almost as soon as the deal was signed, there was a transformation in that situation. It was as if debt reduction, however small, was a signal to the financial markets to reassess the debtor countries. And suddenly Third World countries, under the new name of "emerging markets," were regarded as attractive places to invest. By 1993 Mexico and Argentina were attracting capital at a faster rate than they had in the 1970s.

The new flows of capital to developing countries have taken different forms from the previous wave. There is virtually no new lending from banks. Instead, there is a mixture of direct foreign investment by multinational corporations; large-scale investment in "emerging" stock markets; and purchases of private bonds, often brokered by the same firms that sold domestic junk bonds in the United States during the 1980s.

Mexico provides the clearest case. Foreign firms, such as U.S. auto companies, have been building factories in Mexico to produce for the U.S. market. Investors have been buying Mexican stocks—the Mexican stock market rose more than 400 percent in dollar terms between the end of 1988 and the end of 1991. And private Mexican investors, like the group of entrepreneurs building a toll road to service the booming northern region, have been selling bonds abroad. Overall capital inflows, negligible between 1982 and 1989, were expected to reach 8 percent of GDP in 1993.

Why did market sentiment change so rapidly? Part of the answer is that Brady deals satisfied the political need to take a pound of flesh out of creditors, freeing countries to move ahead. Another part of the answer is that some debtor nations have put their own houses in order, balancing budgets, reducing inflation, freeing up their trade and selling off government-owned companies. But capital has started to flow even to countries like Brazil, which has yet to bring its budget or inflation rate under control, let alone put together a serious long-term reform plan.

It's hard to escape the suspicion that there is a strong psychological element to the change of opinion. And one wonders what will come next.

The important point for the U.S. economy, however, is that whatever happens there will not be a replay of the 1982 debt crisis. U.S. banks are no longer heavily exposed in the Third World, and the sums of money involved are simply not large enough to make much of a difference to our economy as a whole.

The G7 and policy coordination

In 1985, at a famous meeting at the Plaza Hotel, finance ministers from the five largest industrial economies met to try to push down the value of the dollar. Somewhat to their own surprise, they succeeded; and as a result consultations between major industrial countries to discuss and in principle coordinate their financial policies became a regular event. The original group of five was extended to include Italy and Canada, creating the Group of Seven, or G7. The G7 now holds annual summits and more frequent meetings of finance ministers.

G7 meetings are lavish affairs that provide excellent photo opportunities, and calls for effective international coordination are a favorite topic for economics writers who want to sound sophisticated and forward-looking. There is at least one well-funded private organization, the G7 Council, that holds conferences simply to discuss G7 affairs. But are G7 meetings—or as afficionados like to call them, the "G7 process"—really important to the United States?

The answer, surprisingly, is probably not.

The economics of interdependence

It sounds on the face of it like a good idea for advanced countries to coordinate their macroeconomic policies. After all, who wants uncoordinated policies? But what, specifically, are the benefits of coordination?

There is a standard argument for coordination, which may be illustrated by the following story: suppose that the industrial world as a whole is in a recession (as in fact it was in 1992). Now suppose that an individual country wants to increase domestic demand in order to get out of the recession. It can do this either by cutting interest rates, to stimulate private investment, or by providing a fiscal stimulus (a tax cut or a public spending increase). But if it moves unilaterally, either policy may get it into trouble. If it tries to expand by cutting interest rates, investors will try to move their money elsewhere in search of higher yields, driving down the value of the country's currency—and this may be inflationary. If it tries to expand using fiscal policy, part of the expansion of demand will fall on imports, leading to a growing trade deficit. So a country may be unwilling to embark on a unilateral policy of trying to end a recession.

But suppose that the major nations can agree to a joint, coordinated expansion. Then the picture is different. If they all cut interest rates together, investors will stay put and nobody's currency will need to fall. Alternatively, if they all engage in fiscal expansion together, each country will see its exports as well as its imports go up, so that trade deficits need not rise, and each country's growth will be reinforced by the stimulus from these higher exports. So the countries may be able to do collectively what none of them is willing to do alone. In principle, then, by agreeing to coordinate their policies, countries can be more effective in dealing with global recessions.

So there is a solid conceptual basis for the idea of internation-al policy coordination. There's only one problem: it just isn't very important in practice, because international trade is of only limited importance to the world's large economies.

The limited importance of coordination

You can get a sense of the limited importance of the G7 process by considering the economic relationships between the United States and the European Community. In absolute terms the two economies do a huge amount of trade. In 1989 the United States exported $85 billion to the EC, and imported approximately the same amount. But these are huge economies, and the trade between them is a surprisingly small fraction of their output: U.S. exports to the EC are less than 2 percent of our GDP.

Now suppose that the EC were to engage in a huge program of spending increases and tax cuts that led to a 10 percent expan-sion in the EC economy. What would this do for the U.S. econo-my?

When an economy recovers from a recession, its imports usu-ally grow more rapidly than its output; the historical ratio is about two to one. So a 10 percent expansion of the EC economy might mean a 20 percent rise in U.S. exports to the EC, which sounds impressive. But since the initial level of exports to the EC is only 2 percent of our GDP, the overall expansionary impact would be only 0.4 percent of GDP—significant, but not of over-whelming importance.

This example involves an expansion program far larger than is ever likely to be negotiated in a G7 meeting. In 1993 Japan agreed to a stimulus package of record size, and even this was expected to raise Japan's GDP by less than 3 percent. Furthermore, Japan would probably have done most of the expansion even without pressure from its G7 partners. The G7 process probably led to a slightly larger Japanese stimulus than would otherwise have happened, and this in turn probably helped expand the U.S. and European economies a little faster than would otherwise have been the case, but it is hard to believe that the net impact on the U.S. economy was more than 0.1 percent of GDP.

The idea of economic policy coordination has attracted a huge amount of economic research over the past decade. There are strong incentives to find reasons why policy coordination is important: it's a glamorous subject, you get to go to fancy meetings, and high officials very much want to hear how much they matter. The conclusion of most studies has, however, been negative. There just isn't much payoff to getting together to set common monetary and fiscal policies.

Does it do any harm?

Even if G7 meetings don't accomplish much, can't they be regarded as a relatively harmless way for officials to spend their time?[14]

Certainly on the scale of things that officials do, international meetings to discuss policy coordination are fairly benign. There are only two risks. The first is simply one of distraction: officials may pay too much attention to glamorous-sounding but unimportant international issues while neglecting domestic priorities. (The United States would have been better off if top officials had paid less attention during the 1980s to Third World debt and more to what has happening to boring domestic savings and loan associations.)

---

14. In 1992 the *Wall Street Journal* ran a very funny pseudo-anthropological report on Multilateral Man, the species who attends international conferences such as G7 meetings. They described him as believing in two propositions: we must cooperate to improve coordination, and coordinate to improve cooperation.

The other risk is that when countries fail to do much to help each other, as they usually will, they will start blaming each other instead. Japan cannot pull the United States out of a recession, or vice versa—but it's not clear that senior officials always understand that, and unrealistic expectations about the benefits from coordination could turn into a new source of international tension.

Europe's monetary woes

International policy coordination is not an important issue for the United States, because there isn't enough interdependence among the big economies to make it one. But this does not mean that international monetary issues are never important. In fact, the early 1990s were marked by a spectacular international monetary drama played out within Europe. The United States was not an active participant in this drama, and it had few direct repercussions for our own economy. Nonetheless, it was such a major part of world events that it seems worth describing briefly.

Why Europe is different

International policy coordination among the big players—the United States, the European Community as a whole, and Japan—is not very important. Within Europe, however, the interdependence of national economic policies has been crucial to understanding events in recent years.

One reason is simply that because Europe is such a compact area, its nations do much more trade with each other than they do with countries on other continents. France's exports to the United States are less than 2 percent of its GDP; its exports to other European Community countries are 15 percent of GDP. Thus the French economy is much more strongly affected by the

economic policies of its neighboring countries than by the policies of Japan or the United States. The rationale for coordination
described earlier is much more important within Europe than
for the global economy as a whole.

In the 1980s this natural interdependence was greatly reinforced by the decision of all major European countries to link
their monetary policies in the European Monetary System.

The European Monetary System or EMS was founded in 1979.
Its initial purpose was to limit the fluctuations of exchange rates
within Europe, fluctuations that had allegedly been creating
unnecessary uncertainty for business.[15] On paper, it is simply an
agreement to stabilize exchange rates within a set of agreed
ranges. For example, at the time of writing there is a "central
parity" of 3.36 French francs per German mark; if the actual
exchange rate goes either above or below that rate by 2.25 percent, France and Germany are supposed to buy or sell each
others' currencies to keep it from going any further. Countries
cannot change their central parities unilaterally: they must meet
and agree with the other members of the system on a new set of
parities.

In practice, the EMS is much more than an exchange rate
arrangement. It is not possible for a government to stabilize an
exchange rate for very long simply by intervening on the foreign
exchange market. Suppose that a country tries simultaneously to
have an expansionary domestic monetary policy and support
the value of its currency. By reducing domestic interest rates it
will provide investors with an incentive to move money out of
the country. If it then tries to support its currency by buying it on
the foreign exchange market, it is trying to undo with its left
hand what it is doing with its right. In practice, a commitment to

15. There is a technical difference between the EMS, which is the overall treaty, and
the Exchange Rate Mechanism or ERM that obliges countries to stabilize their currencies. At the time of writing, the United Kingdom remains a member of the EMS
but not of the ERM. This legalistic point will be ignored in the text.

stabilize the exchange rate must be backed by the willingness to raise interest rates to defend the currency.

So the EMS in effect linked the monetary policies of European countries together. But how were these policies coordinated? As a practical matter, Europe took its lead from Germany.

The German hegemony

In the early 1980s Europe, like the United States, was suffering from serious inflation. All of the major countries had made fighting inflation a priority. Germany had, however, the best reputation as a diligent inflation-fighter. The German central bank, the Bundesbank, has more independence than its counterparts in France, Italy, and the United Kingdom. Also, the hyperinflation of 1920–23 remains a strong German memory. So Germany was known to be willing to pay the price of fighting inflation.

In this situation the European Monetary System was very useful to governments whose records on inflation were not as good: it offered an opportunity to hitch a ride on German credibility. By matching German monetary policy and thus pegging the value of the franc to that of the mark, French policymakers could hope to convince bond markets, labor unions, and others that they were really serious about getting inflation under control. The same was true for Italy and eventually for Spain and the United Kingdom; smaller European countries like Denmark and the Netherlands naturally fell into line. In effect, all of Europe voluntarily adopted German monetary leadership as a way of proving its commitment to stable prices.

It's worth pointing out that German leadership was not the result of overwhelming economic dominance. Germany is the largest economy in Europe, but its GDP is only about 25 percent larger than that of France, the next largest, and it accounts for only 28 percent of the GDP of the European Community as a whole. Germany could not have ruled Europe's money if it had not been a big economy—try to imagine a Dutch monetary hegemony—but its leadership was not inevitable.

Nonetheless, the tacit arrangement under which Germany controlled Europe's money worked very well as long as German interests and those of the rest of Europe coincided. From 1982 until 1990, fighting inflation was everyone's main priority, and leadership by the stern Bundesbank was widely accepted.

Then came the big shock: the reunification of West and East Germany in 1989.

German reunification and the breakup of the EMS

When East Germany emerged from communist rule, it turned out that the economy was a mess. Productivity was low, factories were antiquated, and there were huge needs for investment in infrastructure and environmental cleanup. It quickly became apparent that the West German economy would need to start running large budget deficits to pay for the rebuilding of the East.

Now these large budget deficits tended to raise demand in West Germany, which could be inflationary. In order to offset this inflation risk, the Bundesbank raised interest rates—a sensible policy from Germany's point of view.

The rise in German interest rates, however, caused serious problems for the rest of Europe. In order to stay within the EMS, countries like France or the United Kingdom were obliged to match Germany's tight money without getting the benefits of Germany's fiscal stimulus. The paradoxical result was that the cost of Germany's reunification ended up producing a recession, not in Germany, but in the rest of Europe.

The logical answer should have been a realignment of parities, raising the value of the mark in terms of other European currencies. But policymakers, who had heavily invested their credibility in the defense of stable exchange rates, were reluctant to contemplate such a realignment. From 1990 until September of 1992, Europe more or less drifted, hoping that the strains on the system would somehow go away.

Finally the system cracked. As the recession in the United Kingdom deepened, political pressure on that country's government increased. Speculators, guessing that the pound might be devalued, began pulling money out of the United Kingdom, forcing the British government to spend huge sums trying to maintain its currency's value. After spending $30 billion in a few days, the British gave up on September 17, dropping out of the EMS and allowing the pound to float. Italy did the same, and several other European countries were forced to devalue.

Interestingly but predictably, the breakup of the EMS immediately reduced the effective linkage among the European economies. By the summer of 1993 the United Kingdom was well on the way to recovery, while France and for that matter Germany itself seemed to be slipping deeper into recession.

Lessons for the United States

The United States has been a largely disinterested bystander to European monetary affairs. But what do we learn from the events?

First, the contrasts between the situation within Europe and the situation in the world economy as a whole are a reminder of the limits to international policy coordination. Europe and Japan will not, for the forseeable future, be as important to the U.S. economy as European nations are to each other.

Second, we see that even within Europe the strong interdependence of the last few years had more to do with politics—the commitment to stabilize exchange rates against the mark—than with any economic logic that forced European economies to move in lockstep. Again, it is hard to see any parallel at a global level.

The subject of global finance is fascinating, and it holds a strong attraction for economic pundits and policymakers alike. The bottom line for the United States is, however, that it is surprisingly irrelevant to our domestic problems.

V

American Prospects

Americans no longer expect much from their economy or from the politicians who manage it. They appear to be satisfied so long as disaster is avoided and most people's living standards do not decline. And the most likely forecast for the 1990s is that Americans will get what they expect—no disaster, but not much good news, either.

Nonetheless, there are other possibilities. Anyone who confidently predicts what the next decade will be like is either foolish or dishonest, for if we learn anything from recent history it is how completely wrong expectations can be. In 1947 most economists were pessimists, expecting the return of mass unemployment. The extraordinary growth of the next 25 years surprised them all. In the early 1970s, by contrast, nearly everyone was excessively optimistic. None of the major economic difficulties of the 1970s and 1980s—the energy crisis, the productivity slowdown, the rise of European unemployment, the debt crisis—was foreseen. So history teaches us to be humble and to entertain a variety of possibilities.

The final part of this book sketches three scenarios: one in which everything works out just fine; one in which the irresponsible policies of the 1980s produce disaster in the 1990s; and finally a sort of central case in which we merely drift along, experiencing neither disaster nor striking success.

Two points should be emphasized about these scenarios. First, they represent an attempt to stay within the range of the plausible. Something wonderful or terrible could always happen—cold fusion could turn out to work, or the spread of AIDS could turn into a crippling burden. The scenarios presented here, however, are all based on relatively reasonable assumptions.

Second, these are scenarios, not forecasts. Looking back from the year 2013, we will surely marvel at our stupidity in 1993. We will wonder how we could have failed to notice these developments that would be crucial in the years ahead (spectacular economic growth in liberalized Eastern Europe and Russia? a super savings and loan crisis as other hidden government liabilities come to light?) In short, these scenarios are illustrations of the kinds of things that might happen, not predictions of what will happen.

15   Happy Ending

The race is not to the swift, nor yet the battle to the strong, nor yet bread to the wise, nor yet flourishing economies to policy-makers of understanding. It is perfectly possible that the American economy will, over the next decade, deliver a level of performance that will make our current anxieties look foolish and perhaps persuade our leaders that they were somehow responsible.

The key is productivity. If productivity growth in the United States were to recover to something like its rates of the 1950s and 1960s, practically everything would fall into place.

A productivity revival?

It's not too hard to make a case that productivity growth in the 1990s will be much better than it was in the 1970s or 1980s. In fact, there are at least four schools of productivity optimists: statistical, generational, managerial, and technological.

The statistical case for a productivity revival starts from the one sure fact in all of this: We don't know much about why productivity growth varies. In particular, we really don't know why productivity grew rapidly from 1945 to 1973, then very slowly thereafter. Since we don't know why growth slowed, we cannot confidently argue that it might not speed up again.

The history of U.S. productivity growth in the twentieth century can be read as encouraging. Looking back at the 10-year average rates of productivity growth shown in Figure 6, we see that this rate has fluctuated around 2 percent, sometimes more, sometimes less. Never mind why: Suppose that it turns out that the 1950s and 1960s were just a lucky draw, and the 1970s and 1980s a bad one. There is no reason that the 1990s shouldn't be another good draw, with productivity growth above 2 percent—and perhaps as high as 3 percent. Judging from the figure, that's well within the range of the possible.

The technological argument for a productivity revival occurs to almost anyone who reads the "science and technology" section of his favorite business magazine. Technologically, the past 15 years have been a parade of wonders: Especially in computation, but also in communication (remember life before the fax?), there has been one revolution after another, with new areas such as biotechnology now seemingly on the verge of widespread practical implementation. Yet economically, the news has been generally dreary—a typical American worker can buy less with his pay today than his father could when Richard Nixon was first inaugurated.

Something is out of kilter here. Either technology isn't all it's cracked up to be, or we haven't yet seen the impact of the new technology on our economy. Maybe the next decade will see businesses learn how to use computers, faxes, and fiberoptics to do something really useful, and the rate of growth will pick up. The highest rate of U.S. productivity growth before the 1950s was in the 1920s, driven by the automobile industry—even though automobiles had been in existence and even in fairly widespread use since the turn of the century. We are arguably in the same situation with regard to personal computers: They are around, but only now are we about to use them creatively to transform our lives.

The managerial argument for rapid growth is something that we already encountered in the discussion of corporate finance. Suppose that Michael Jensen is largely right, and that most of the gains from takeovers and buyouts reflect increases in economic efficiency as lax management is either replaced or given incentives to serve investor interests. And suppose that it is really true that people such as Michael Milken have developed an organizational form for the modern firm that will allow productive restructuring throughout the economy. Then the takeover-buyout boom of the 1980s may turn out to be the prologue to a period of rapid productivity growth.

Lastly, the generational argument for accelerating growth simply points out that the 1960s are receding into the past. If you think that the ultimate source of the productivity problem lies in the fact that too many talented people dropped out, wasted years trying to become social workers, and/or avoided entrepreneurial or corporate careers because of misplaced idealism, then you would expect to see faster growth as the success-oriented post–baby-boom generation makes its way into the work force.

None of these arguments is conclusive. In particular, it is possible to make a compelling case that America's social problems—the growth of the underclass, and the decline of educational quality and achievement even among middle-class children—will drag down our productivity growth even further. But the truth is that nobody knows.

If the optimists are right, and productivity growth does accelerate, when will the good news start to come in? The answer is that the good times may already have begun.

Ironically, the first signs of something good happening began during a recession that so dismayed the American people that a once-popular president was booted out of office. Measured the usual way, by the point at which the output of the U.S. economy began rising, an economic recovery actually started in 1991.

Unemployment continued to rise until mid-1992, however, because there was a surprise surge in the rate of productivity growth. In 1992 productivity grew at a startling 2.8 percent per year, its best performance since 1972.

Did this represent a fundamental turnaround in performance? Pessimists argued that any productivity gain would be a one-time event: U.S. companies were simply responding to a prolonged recession with savage cuts in their work forces. And they worried that layoffs of workers with once-secure jobs would create a new class of long-term unemployed, in effect raising the NAIRU. These pessimistic fears were not unreasonable: something like that seems to have happened in Great Britain, where a deep recession was followed in the mid-1980s by several years of surging productivity, but where the productivity boom seems to have run its course and unemployment remains stubbornly high.

On the other hand, some industry observers thought they saw the beginnings of a real productivity revolution.

The consequences of a productivity boom

Suppose that the optimists turn out to be right, and that U.S. productivity grows much faster in the decade ahead than it did in the past 15 years—say, at close to 3 percent a year. How would this affect the economy?

The answer is that it would make many, but not all, of the problems discussed in this book fade away.

To begin with, rapid productivity growth would lead to a general rise in living standards. If productivity were to grow as fast in the 1990s as it did in the 1960s, the average American worker's take-home pay would grow by something like 30 percent. Unless there were an extraordinary further increase in inequality, this growth in income would be widely shared. As a result, the era of growing misery at the bottom of the income scale would be over.

Faster productivity growth would also do a great deal to defuse the problem of the trade deficit through a variety of indirect channels. First, faster growth would raise tax revenues. While some demands on the public purse would also grow more rapidly (like demands for increased infrastructure investment), others—notably defense and interest on the public debt—would not. So the budget deficit would fade away, and as a consequence the national savings rate would rise, contributing to a decline in the trade deficit.

At the same time, faster growth would minimize the consequences of trade deficits. While claims of foreigners on the U.S. economy would continue to rise (at least for a while), they would be a smaller piece of a larger pie and would thus create less of a drain. And a U.S. economy that was doing relatively well would probably experience less conflict with Japan, even if Japan were doing still better.

Faster productivity growth would not, of course, solve every economic problem, and it may be useful to remind ourselves of what it would not do. It would not necessarily reduce the unemployment rate: America did very well at containing unemployment during the 1970s and 1980s, despite low productivity growth, while Europe did badly, despite substantially faster productivity growth. It would not necessarily help reduce inflation: Inflation in the U.S. first took off in the high-growth 1960s and was brought largely under control in the low-growth 1980s. It would not even protect the economy form the risks of financial crisis: Both the 1929 crash and the 1982 Latin American debt crisis followed decades of unusually high productivity growth in their victims.

Still, it is important to realize that a spontaneous productivity revival that would not be out of line with past experience could solve most of the pressing economic issues facing the United States without any positive action from our leadership. We could simply get lucky. On a purely unscientific basis, I would assign this kind of happy ending a probability of 20 percent.

Hard Landing

Despite the general contentment of the American public with
their country's economic performance, predictions of catastrophe—doomsday books—still do a brisk business. While most of
these predictions (the ones that sell best) are pure fantasy, there
is a widespread undercurrent of concern that somehow the
excesses of the 1980s—the budget deficit, the trade deficit, the
growth of corporate debt—have prepared the ground for a
future crisis.

Where might such a crisis come from? Popular books on economic crisis usually draw their images from 1929: a collapse of
business confidence leading to global financial collapse. But a
1929-style crisis is quite unlikely in the modern world, for reasons to be discussed in a moment. A better bet is a crisis arising
from the U.S. trade deficit and growing foreign debt—a crisis on
Latin American lines.

1929 again?

The image of 1929 still haunts many Americans: the bubble of
optimism suddenly bursts, stockbrokers leap from windows,
prosperity vanishes almost overnight. Can it happen again?

It depends on what you mean. Can a stock market crash like
that of 1929 happen again? Yes, of course it can—in fact, it

already has. The initial fall in U.S. stock prices in the 1987 crash was as large as that of 1929, and the collapse spread around the world faster and more thoroughly. Could such a crash generate another depression? No. It didn't in 1987, and it almost surely won't the next time it happens.

By purely financial measures, the crash of 1987 was every bit as bad as the initial financial panic in 1929. The initial fall in the U.S. stock prices was slightly larger in 1929; but in 1987 the U.S. fall was much more nearly matched by the decline abroad. So on a global basis Black Monday in 1987 was actually worse than Black Thursday in 1929.

But from that point on the stories diverge totally. The initial crash in 1929 was followed by a deepening recession and by successive waves of further stock decline. The 1987 crash was followed by relatively rapid economic growth and a corresponding recovery of stock prices that soon erased virtually all of the initial drop.

Why didn't 1987 play like 1929? The basic answer is a surprising one, given today's widespread cynicism about economic policy and the role of government: We've learned something since 1929, and the Federal Reserve used that knowledge effectively. Stock market crashes need not cause severe downturns in the real economy. The crash in 1929 helped intensify a recession that was already developing. Even a year later that recession seemed unpleasant, but not menacing. What really turned the crash into the Depression was the collapse of the banking system in 1931, which led to a huge contraction in the availability of credit. In the judgment of most of those who have studied the events, this banking collapse was simply unnecessary. It happened only because of the almost eerie passivity of the Federal Reserve, which failed to do anything to stop it, permitting massive deflation and monetary collapse in the early 1930s.

In 1987 the Federal Reserve chose not to repeat its previous mistake. Faced with the stock crash, it rapidly expanded the supply of base money. The rest is already history. Instead of a Depression, there was faster growth in the year following the crash than in the year before. Indeed, the 1987 crash may actually have improved the economy's performance by leading to a rise in the personal savings rate. The Fed demonstrated that it is not only possible but easy to insulate the real economy from a financial panic.

Of course a misguided or incompetent Federal Reserve could still manage to turn some future stock crash into something serious. On a true gold standard, for example, or with a rigid monetarist rule in effect, the Federal Reserve would have been unable to carry out the rapid credit expansion of late 1987. Given reasonably competent and flexible management, however, there does not seem to be any reason to expect a repeat of 1929.

A U.S. debt crisis?

It is the spring of 1995, and the deterioration of the U.S. trade position predicted by many economists has proceeded faster than expected: First-quarter numbers indicate a trade deficit running at an annual rate of more than $250 billion. At the same time, inflation has gradually accelerated to about a 6 percent annual rate, and the Federal Reserve has tightened its policy in an effort to rein in the price rise, leading to a mild recession that has raised unemployment to 7 percent. The combination of a widening trade gap and the recession lead to widespread layoffs of manufacturing workers.

The trade gap also contributes to a growing mood of economic nationalism, fed both by trade and by the never-ending stream of conspicuous sales of U.S. real estate and firms to foreign nationals. Ross Perot has made economic nationalism a key plank in his campaign. The large sums accepted from Japanese sources by former high government officials, while generally legal, add to the bad taste left by the 1994 influence-buying scandal. Pollsters tell Perot that the Japan issue can win the election for him, and tell the incumbents that they must act extra tough on Japan to counteract a public perception that they are soft on foreign economic interests.

In this highly flammable situation, the spark comes from the auto industry. Large-scale entry into the U.S. market by Japanese firms, who in 1995 produce almost 5 million cars and trucks in the United States, has led to substantial overcapacity; this overcapacity becomes severe when the recession and rising imports cut into domestic shipments. When General Motors announces a number of plant closings, blaming competition from Japanese firms producing here, there are widespread calls for limits on foreign ownership. When one of the major Japanese manufacturers itself announces that it is closing one of its U.S. plants, however, there is an overwhelming demand for restrictions not only on the ability of foreign firms to invest in the United States but also on their freedom to pull their money out.

Analysts later agree that it was the combination of fears of confiscatory U.S. policies toward foreign investment and worries about the U.S. trade deficit that started wholesale capital flight in the late spring. The dollar quickly drops to 80 yen. There it is briefly stabilized by a combination of large Treasury purchases of dollars on the foreign exchange market, financed by short-term loans from the governments of Germany and Japan, and 15 percent interest rates that attract some short-term private funds. But attempts to regain the confidence of foreign long-term investors are unsuccessful, not least because the few major acquisitions of U.S. firms that take place are widely denounced as "fire sales" due to the weak dollar.

At this point, there is a crucial policy error. As a severe recession looms on the verge of an election, the Federal Reserve loses its nerve and temporarily loosens policy. This move proves disastrous: The dollar drops to 60 yen, and inflation, thanks in part to the global oil crisis, accelerates within a year to more than 20 percent. The subsequent IMF-supervised stabilization program drives unemployment to 13 percent in 1998, and U.S. industrial output does not regain its 1995 level until 2001. . . .

This is a fairly lurid fantasy—but not wildly unreasonable. The United States might run a current account deficit of $150 billion two years from now. A loss of confidence by international investors could easily force the United States to move into a current account surplus, potentially requiring a reduction in U.S. domestic demand relative to output of as much as 4 to 5 percent. The associated fall in the dollar would reduce U.S. real income by several additional percentage points. Put it all together and it becomes plausible that we could face a shock more severe than either the 1973 or the 1979 oil shocks. Each of those shocks sent inflation into double digits; the 1979 shock also sent unemployment above 10 percent and precipitated the massive recession of the early 1980s.

In 1985 Stephen Marris of the Institute for International Economics laid out a scenario for a "hard landing" based on a collapse of investor confidence in the dollar. When the dollar began sliding, right on schedule, Marris's prophecy seemed to be coming true. But the dollar slide did both much less harm and much less good than Marris had imagined: The trade deficit remained stubbornly high, but the inflationary impact was also mild. As the dollar stabilized in 1987, and eventually began to strengthen again, the hard landing scenario began to lose followers. A growing body of opinion claims that a hard landing of the sort Marris described cannot happen.

The optimism that has now become conventional wisdom has two components: a belief that the United States will continue to receive foreign financing for as long as it needs it; and a belief that even if foreigners do become reluctant to invest in the

United States, leading to a decline of the dollar, no serious adverse effects will result. This conventional wisdom is probably right. But the truth is that we don't really know; just because Marris's hard landing hasn't happened yet doesn't mean that it can't happen.

Prospects for foreign financing

The United States is the world's largest debtor and continues to sell assets to foreigners at a near-record pace. Why should anyone think that this can go on almost indefinitely?

There are at least four reasons now being widely advanced to justify the belief that we can continue to finance massive current account deficits for many years to come. One of these reasons is a good point. The other three are just wrong.

The good point is that while U.S. foreign debt and its current account deficit are huge, so is the U.S. economy—and the dollar value of U.S. output increases over time due to both real growth and inflation. As a result, even deficits and debts that sound inconceivably large may not be overwhelming burdens. Suppose, for example, that the United States continues to run current account deficits at the rate of $150 billion every year for the next decade, so that by the year 2000 our net foreign investment position is a negative $2.5 trillion. This sounds like an impossible sum. Yet if growth and inflation continue at recent rates, this would be less than 20 percent of GNP, and the net investment income of foreigners in the United States would be well within our ability to pay.

Matters will, of course, look different if the current account deficit widens instead of stabilizing; but it remains true that when the deficit is expressed as a share of national income instead of as a raw number, the instinctive reaction that the United States is on a wildly unsustainable course becomes hard to justify.

So much for the good reason not to worry about continued financing. What about the bad reasons?

One widely expressed view is that America will not have any financing problems because, even with rapid growth in U.S. foreign debt, claims on America will remain a small part of the portfolios of international investors. This is the argument offered in a recent report by the Bank for International Settlements (BIS), which concludes that since the share of claims on the United States in international portfolios will remain modest, "the financing of further large deficits on the current account of the U.S. balance of payments through inflows of foreign private capital need not lead to major financial market disturbances in the coming years."

Unfortunately, while it is true that claims on the United States will not be an overwhelming share of world portfolios in the next five or even ten years, it is also irrelevant. After all, claims on Mexico and Brazil never became large parts of world portfolios either; that didn't prevent a Latin American debt crisis. The point is that it is not the ratio of claims on the United States to the rest of the world's assets that matters—it is the ratio of those claims to the expected ability and/or willingness of the United States to pay.

A second bad argument is that the United States has a special position because of the international role of the dollar. In much of the world, the dollar serves as a unit of account: Much international trade is invoiced in dollars, much international lending and borrowing is denominated in dollars, and much international liquidity takes the form of dollar accounts. The argument is that this somehow means that the rest of the world automatically finances our deficits.

There are two things wrong with this view. First, it takes the special role of the dollar for granted. But in fact the outlines of emerging European and Japanese currency blocs can already be seen; this will surely cut into the dollar's special role. More important, the fact that the U.S. dollar is widely used as a unit of account does not mean that people around the world are obliged to accept dollar bills that the United States prints, or to put money into the U.S. economy. If a Japanese bank makes a loan to Turkey, payable in U.S. dollars, the use of the dollar is simply a convenience. Nobody has to put money in the United States. Dollar bank accounts do not necessarily have much to do with the United States. You can get a Eurodollar account in London, and if you withdraw your money, you get dollars. But, like any bank, the bank in London will carry only a limited reserve of dollars, investing most of its deposits wherever it sees the highest return. Even a bank account in the United States need not help finance the U.S. current account deficit, except to the limited extent that reserves have to be held. Money deposited in a bank in New York is just as likely to be lent abroad as money placed in banks in London or Singapore.

Suppose that investors around the world begin to doubt whether the United States will remain willing to service its foreign debt, or to allow foreign firms in the United States to send as much of their profits home as they like. Will the fact that the dollar is an international currency somehow prevent capital flight from the United States? Of course not.

The most recent argument for not worrying about the dollar is the growing tendency of foreigners to invest in the United States by buying real estate and firms, rather than debt. To many observers this seems to eliminate worries about debt service. To quote the BIS study again, "foreign direct investment . . . does not constitute external debt the servicing of which represents a fixed charge." But foreign firms are not investing here for their health. A dollar invested in the United States will eventually generate profits that accrue to those foreign owners. Since direct investment typically yields a higher rate of return than simple lending, the eventual cost to U.S. residents of a dollar invested directly will be larger than the cost of a dollar borrowed. If we think that the eventual constraint on U.S. foreign debt will be doubts about our willingness rather than our ability to repay them, it is worth bearing in mind that foreign-owned real estate and factories are even better targets for economic nationalism than foreign-owned bonds.

In sum, there is really only one valid argument in support of the belief that the United States can go on running current account deficits: the argument that a huge and growing U.S. economy can take on a massive debt load without really becoming overburdened.

But there is a reason not to feel entirely comfortable with this argument, either: the experience of the Latin American nations. During the 1970s, and right up to the edge of the crisis, the general verdict of economists was that the growth of Latin debt did not represent a problem, because part of the real value of the debt was eroded by inflation and the rest of the borrowing was being used to finance growth. In April 1981, to take a representative example, Harvard economist Jeffrey Sachs wrote that "much of the growth in LDC debt reflects increased investment and should not pose a problem of repayment . . . This is particularly true of Brazil and Mexico." Only 16 months later Mexico announced that it was stopping payments on its debt; Sachs himself became the leading advocate of large-scale cancellation of Third World debt.

Nor was it only economists who failed to perceive the seriousness of debt growth in Latin America; virtually no one foresaw the problem. In the survey of country risk analysts published by Institutional Investor in April 1982—only four months before the Mexican payment stoppage—the Latin debtors received reasonably good grades, with Mexico actually rated above South Korea.

As a matter of pure economics, the United States could continue to run deficits at the current rate for the next ten years without putting itself into an unsustainable position—and there is a good chance that it will get away with doing just that. But as foreign ownership of U.S. assets continues to grow, economic nationalism in the United States will increase. This will make foreigners justifiably nervous about the security of their investments. If this nationalism gets out of hand—or even if foreigners think that it might get out of hand—there will be capital flight from the United States that could quickly spiral, Latin American–style, into a full-fledged balance of payment crisis. The further the United States gets into debt, the larger this risk becomes. So a cutoff of foreign financing sometime during the 1990s remains a real possibility.

But this is only half of the hard-landing story. The scenario calls not only for capital flight and a plunging dollar but for disastrous macroeconomic effects as well. Are these likely?

Macroeconomics of crisis

If foreigners lose confidence in the United States, the immediate impact will be a fall in the dollar. But so what? From early 1985 to early 1987 the dollar lost roughly half its value in terms of the yen and the mark. Yet this slow-motion financial crash did no more damage than the fast-forward fall in stock prices that followed. Unemployment continued to decline; inflation accelerated only slightly. If stock market panics don't have tocause recessions, isn't the same true of foreign exchange market panics?

Not necessarily. When the stock market crashes, an active Federal Reserve can turn the crash into a purely paper event with no real consequences. If foreigners lose confidence in the United States, by contrast, there is an unavoidable real adjustment: We have to start spending no more than we earn. Nothing the Federal Reserve can do will force foreigners to continue to finance the U.S. current account deficit if they are unwilling to do so.

Can this real adjustment be made smoothly? The experience of the 1970s and 1980s is not encouraging. The 1982 debt crisis in Latin America derailed growth in that region for the rest of the decade. The oil crises of 1973 and 1979 represented shocks similar to a hypothetical hard landing for the dollar; they produced sharp inflationary spikes and deep recessions both at home and abroad. The only encouraging experience is that of the decline of the dollar from 1985 to 1987. And there are several reasons for doubting that this experience will be repeated.

First, what happened from 1985 to 1987 was not a full-fledged cutoff of capital inflows to the United States. Instead, as the dollar declined investors eventually became convinced that U.S. assets were cheap at current prices, and the dollar stabilized without having to fall enough to balance U.S. trade. In fact, the U.S. current account deficit, and hence the need for foreign financing, continued to grow for two years after the dollar started falling, due to lagged effects of the dollar's previous rise. Even in 1989 foreign capital inflows were about 2.5 percent of GNP, compared with 3.4 percent in 1986. Contrast this with Mexico, where a cutoff of foreign lending forced the country to move from a trade deficit of 2 percent of GNP in 1981 to a trade surplus of 5 percent in 1984, and we see that the United States has not yet known what it means to face the music.

Second, the fact that the decline of the dollar came immediately after an equally rapid rise dampened the effect on U.S. inflation. The strong dollar had not, by early 1985, been fully reflected in import prices. When the dollar rose, many foreign firms didn't cut their dollar prices, they simply increased their profit margins. As a result, when the dollar fell they could absorb a substantial part of that fall by cutting into their profit margins. Japanese firms in particular absorbed about half of the yen's rise by cutting their export prices relative to the prices they charged domestic customers. This response may have frustrated U.S.

firms hoping that the lower dollar would help them win back markets, but it helped prevent any inflationary surge in the United States.

Also helping to hold down inflation was good luck on world raw material markets. The price of oil crashed in 1985, just as the dollar fell, offsetting inflationary pressures; other raw material prices fell to new lows in real terms. In 1978 and 1979 a falling dollar interacted with soaring raw material prices to produce an inflationary surge. In the years since 1985 the U.S. economy has had much better luck.

Lastly, the fall of the dollar took place at a time when the U.S. economy was operating with some slack capacity and with declining inflationary expectations. That meant that any pain from reduced foreign funding could be more than offset by increased output, as the Federal Reserve allowed the unemployment rate to fall from 7 to 5.3 percent.

If you want to envision a real hard landing, simply imagine that each of these factors is reversed. Suppose that foreigners face a perceived risk that is not alleviated by a lower dollar— such as fears of expropriation. Suppose that the resulting dollar crash follows a period of dollar stability, so there is no cushion to brake the rise in import prices, and that we have the bad luck (or lack of foresight) to stumble into a third oil crisis just as the dollar plunges. And suppose that the U.S. economy is already having an inflation problem when the crisis hits. What you get is a recipe for a truly disastrous hard landing.

This hard-landing scenario could happen, but it doesn't have to, even if policy continues to drift. Foreigners probably will continue to finance our deficits; even if they don't, we might handle the situation well enough to avoid a crisis. I give the hard landing a 25 percent chance of happening.

17   Drift

This final scenario is the one that comes closest to a forecast. It describes a U.S. economy in which tomorrow is much like today: in which there are no radical developments, either favorable or unfavorable, that make the economy of the 1990s very different from that of the late 1980s. In this scenario economic policy continues much as it has, with no major departures.

There are some countries for which this kind of scenario would be patently absurd. In a country like Peru, to take an extreme example, one can look at the evaporating foreign exchange reserves and declare that either a massive change in policies or a slide into anarchy must occur within a few months. The United States is not in that kind of situation. There is nothing in the basic arithmetic of U.S. budget deficits, foreign debt, or inflation that would prevent us from continuing more or less with current policies for another decade.

So let us suppose that the United States manages to drift along with no radical departures. What might the economy look like?

The domestic economy

The most likely forecast for the U.S. domestic economy in the 1990s is that it will look a lot like 1988–1989: fairly slow growth, modestly rising incomes for most Americans, generally good employment performance, a gradual acceleration of inflation.

If U.S. productivity growth does not accelerate, U.S. economic growth will actually have to slow down a little in the 1990s. The reason is demographic: The baby boomers are all now in the work force, and the great increase in female participation will probably not continue at the same rate. So in this central scenario we would see the U.S. economy grow at an average of slightly more than 2 percent a year over the next decade.

Median family income, however, probably would do little better than in the 1980s, partly because the number of families will not grow as fast, and partly because we would not expect the rising income of the most affluent to siphon off as much of the total growth in income as it did in the Reagan years. So the average family might gain about 10 percent in real income over the course of the decade. Assuming that the widening of the gap between highly skilled and less skilled workers will not continue, the 1990s will also differ from the 1980s in showing some rise in income for many of the poor. At the very bottom, however, everything we know points to a growing and ever more miserable underclass; the number of truly desperate poor will grow, as will the associated social pathologies. In other words, the middle class will probably do better in the 1990s than in the 1980s, but the ugly contrast between great affluence for one minority and intense poverty for another should be even greater in the year 2000.

Meanwhile, unemployment probably will drift down, as the economy recovers from the 1990-92 recession.

As for inflation, it seems clear that the country does not want to pay the price of a serious drive to stabilize prices. And if the continual pressure on the Federal Reserve to avoid even a slight recession is any guide, our leaders appear prepared to take more risks on the side of inflation than on the side of recession. The rule seems to be that when the Fed thinks there might be a recession, but isn't sure, it is under pressure to loosen policy just in case; when it thinks that inflation may be picking up, but isn't sure, it is expected to wait and see before tightening. This implies a persistent bias toward higher inflation. It would not be surprising if inflation has crept up to 7 percent by the end of the decade. Given what we have said about the costs of inflation, however, this will do almost no real harm.

The international economy

If the domestic U.S. economy in the year 2000 may look fairly similar to its current state, the international economy—and the role of the United States in that international economy—will almost surely look quite different.

In the first place, foreigners will own quite a lot of America. Net foreign claims on the United States will be something like 20 percent of GNP, with interest and dividends on these claims nearly 2 percent of national income. More strikingly, foreign-owned corporations will play a big role in the U.S. economy. It would not be surprising if, by the year 2000, foreign firms account for 25 percent of U.S. manufacturing production and own 45 percent of our banking sector.

This widespread foreign ownership will be a blow to traditional views of America's place in the world, a blow reinforced by the realities of international economic influence. By the year 2000, an increasingly unified Europe will have a larger GNP than America's, and Japan will have a GNP that in dollar terms is 80 percent or more of the U.S. level. Both Europe and Japan will have substantially larger exports than the United States, and both will have larger overseas investment—Japan in particular. So by many measures the United States will have sunk to the number-three economic power in the world. We will still be the leading military power, but this will be little cause for satisfaction.

The risk of nationalistic U.S. reaction in these circumstances—Gary Shilling's shift from Star Wars to Trade Wars—is obvious. If we fail to rise above our instincts, and if the Europeans and the Japanese follow suit, the 1990s will see a steady growth of trade restrictions. There may be no open rupture of the existing trade treaties, but they will be bypassed in various ways. The world will therefore tend to break apart into three trading blocs: North American, European, and East Asian. In this, at least, the near future will be different from the recent past: The effects of trade restrictions should be enough to reverse the trend of growing international economic integration. At least as far as trade goes, the world economy is likely to be *less* unified in the year 2000 than it is today.

Can this happen? Don't modern technologies of transportation and communication imply an ever more integrated world economy, whatever governments may do? History tells us otherwise. Economic nationalism can easily reverse the long-term trend toward a more integrated world economy for decades at a time.

Consider what happened to world trade for much of the twentieth century. We tend to assume that world economy is something that needs widebody jets and fax machines. But the truth is that these technologies are minor improvements from an economic point of view. The really decisive technologies for creating an integrated world economy were steamships, railroads, and telegraphs. These made the costs of shipping goods and transferring information low. Everything since has only further reduced costs that were already low by 1880. By 1913 our great-grandfathers had created an international economy that in many respects—mobility of labor, mobility of long-term capital—was more closely integrated than anything the world has seen since.

Figure 28 shows a useful measure, the ratio of total trade (exports plus imports) to GNP, for Britain and the United States for selected dates since the mid-nineteenth century. The figure reveals that large-scale trade is nothing new; the United Kingdom was more of a trading nation in the reign of Queen Victoria than the United States ever has been or probably ever will be.

The figure also reveals something else: the extraordinary decline in international trade after 1913. There is no mystery about what happened in between: Nationalism and the resulting increase in protectionism depressed trade to much lower levels than technology made possible.

Something similar, although milder, is likely in the years ahead. World trade outside the trading blocs will grow more slowly than world output, and might even shrink in real terms.

This is an unfortunate prospect, but not a terrible one. As pointed out previously, the costs of protectionism are often exaggerated. The kind of fragmentation of global markets envisioned here could reduce world output by 1 percent or possibly even 2

SHARE OF TRADE IN NATIONAL INCOME

Figure 28
The long-term trend toward international integration can be reversed for decades at a time by economic nationalism. Trade was a larger share of both American and British national income before World War I than it was again until the 1970s.

percent from what it otherwise would have been by the end of the century. That is an enormous cost in absolute terms—say, $250 billion a year at current prices—but it would not have a severe negative impact on living standards.

There is one major tension in this scenario. Suppose that economic nationalism leads to a slowing of growth in world trade. If the United States is to finance its continuing trade deficits, it must continue to attract foreign investment. Yet if current trends persist, foreign ownership will soon be a very conspicuous factor in our economy. What if the same economic nationalism that leads to trade restrictions also scares off foreign investors? Then we go back to our hard-landing scenario.

Barring such a crisis, however, the U.S. economy can live with an increasingly protectionist world; it can even deliver modest increases in living standards to its population.

Looking back at the future

To many Americans this scenario will sound reasonably good. There is no crisis; most people are better off. If the economy actually delivers fairly steady growth at more than 2 percent for the next decade, if inflation remains in single digits, if unemployment stays at roughly current levels, most people will count the decade a success. There will doubtless be caustic remarks from politicians and journalists about the foolishness of those doomsayers who claimed that the trade and budget deficits would bring catastrophe.

Yet this is a scenario that falls far short of what used to be regarded as successful performance. Twenty-five years ago, it was taken for granted that the rapid productivity growth of the postwar period, and corresponding growth in living standards, would continue. When Herman Kahn and associates examined the prospects for the U.S. economy in their 1967 book *The Year*

2000, their most pessimistic scenario called for 2.5 percent annual productivity growth—and they argued strongly that at least 4 percent was more likely. That same year, in another series of essays on the year 2000, *Fortune* magazine projected that real wages by then would climb by 150 percent.

Imagine confronting these forecasters with a nation where productivity increased little more than 1 percent a year, where real hourly wages fell through the 1970s and 1980s, where poverty grew in absolute terms. They would have regarded such an outcome as a highly implausible disaster. They would also have predicted a drastic political reaction—especially if one added to the story greatly increased wealth at the top of the income distribution, a declining American position in the world, and growing foreign ownership of U.S. assets.

Yet this scenario now looks perfectly acceptable, and might even be regarded as a success. What is truly remarkable about our times is that the political system accepts our reduced prospects with so much equanimity.

In his 1971 novel *Love in the Ruins*, Walker Percy succinctly described the view of the future as it looked in the politically apocalyptic but economically sunny 1960s: "The center did not hold. However, the gross national product continues to rise." He got it exactly wrong. The GNP didn't continue to rise—at least not as fast as we thought it would. But things didn't fall apart, and the center held after all. And given the diminished expectations Americans now have for their economy, that is probably the way it will be for the next decade.

Index